Transitions

Unlocking the Creative Quilter Within

Andrea
Balosky

Credits

Editor-in-Chief .... Kerry I. Hoffman

Technical Editor .... Laura M. Reinstatler

Managing Editor .... Judy Petry

Copy Editors .... Liz McGehee
Melissa Riesland

Illustrator .... Margaret Kanazawa

Technical Illustrator .... Laurel Strand

Photographer .... Brent Kane

Text Designer .... Sandy Wing

Cover Designer .... Kay Green

Production Assistant .... Claudia L'Heureux

Transitions: Unlocking the Creative Quilter Within
©1996 by Andrea Balosky

That Patchwork Place, Inc.
PO Box 118
Bothell, WA 98041-0118 USA

Printed in Hong Kong   01 00 99 98 97 96   6 5 4 3 2 1

Library of Congress Cataloging-in-Publication Data
Balosky, Andrea,
    Transitions : unlocking the creative quilter within /
Andrea Balosky.
        p.   cm.
    ISBN 1-56477-170-9
    1. Patchwork quilts—Design. 2. Inspiration. I. Title.
TT835.B295   1996
746.46—dc20   96-26498
                                                                      CIP

Dedication

I dedicate this book to my parents, whose love and faith fostered my curiosity, bolstered my independence, and prepared me for adventures. Also, to my brother and my husband. Life is sweeter because of them.

Acknowledgments

I thank That Patchwork Place for their courage. This book is a departure, but was met with enthusiasm and encouragement.

I thank P & B Textiles for their beautiful fabric.

I thank Jane L. Poole, senior editor of *Opera News*, for providing me with archival extracts about Casa di Riposo.

For their love, friendship, and inspiration: The Douchettes, Laura D'Alessandro, Janell de Varona, Victoria Bosche, Alexandria Rossoff, John Simpkins, Tetsuro Ushijima, Janit Brockway, Jean Wells, Lorraine Torrence, Dana Ivers, Claudia Law Greenberg, Tonye Phillips, Debbie Myers, and Sheridan Van Dolah.

For their support and encouragement: The Stitchin' Post, The East of the Cascade Quilters, The Sisters and Camp Sherman Post Offices, Hospice of Central Oregon, and the friends and neighbors of Camp Sherman and Sisters who cheered me on.

For the inspiration of their lives and their life's work: Fred Astaire, Albert Einstein, Alan Watts, Alvin Ailey, Billie Holiday, Bob Dylan, Busby Berkeley, Carl Jung, Christopher Alexander, George Balanchine, Georgia O'Keeffe, Giuseppe Verdi, Dame Joan Sutherland, Joseph Campbell, Lao Tzu, Louis Armstrong, Ludwig van Beethoven, Mahatma Gandhi, Marilyn Horne, Martin Luther King, Jr., Maya Angelou, Paul Poiret, Ram Dass, Vincenzo Bellini, Wolfgang Amadeus Mozart, Johannes Sebastian Bach, the Dalai Lama, the Peace Corps, Hospice, and the Public Broadcasting Service.

Table of Contents

Introduction

Why This Book?

I've been making quilts off and on since 1964. Mostly off. In 1992, I decided to make quilting a more significant part of my life. I found myself in a pickle because I wasn't sure how to go about doing this. Being versed enough in quilt basics, I was hoping for something more than just another class.

For research, I started with the bookshelf. There were many books on technique, replete with full-color pictures of wonderful quilts and brimming with detailed instruction. Everything I needed to know about those quilts was furnished on attractive, glossy pages. But I wanted to make *my* quilts, not just duplicate someone else's great idea. I searched through quilt books of another kind: the epic treasuries of our heritage. These, too, were inspiring, but still not quite suited to my needs or nature. I looked through catalogs of major juried competitions, felt awed and inspired, but lame. I was motivated, but lacked practical information.

Between the quilt recipe books on one end of the bookshelf and the dream-quilt books on the other, I stared at a gap. A bit dismayed, I suspected I was expecting the impossible. So, armed with little more than inspiration and gumption, I began. I self-apprenticed. I'm still in apprenticeship. From what I've gleaned thus far, I'll be here for a while, making my way through the many curious turns this journey entails. My induction this year into Quilters Emeritus is probably a remote possibility.

I wrote the book

I couldn't find.

I wrote this book because there must be others who share my original dilemma. Statistically, there are five to twelve million quiltmakers out there. Surely, there are others struggling with or hovering on the brink of independent work.

I admit it is a bit brash, the non-expert giving counsel. I pondered this vantage point and concluded that my nonexpert status is probably a good thing. I still operate within the same context of one adrift in a sea of uncertainty. And though now the seas are far less treacherous and the uncertainty less perplexing, the thrashings of struggle are fresh. What I share is tinged with recent skirmishes and advances, and could be helpful to those who tread similarly.

I wrote the book I couldn't find. Had this book been around a few years ago, I would have pounced on it.

Quiltmakers on the Verge

Although you're joyfully committed to quiltmaking, somewhere in your heart you feel you're ready for something else. Restlessness persists, despite the fact that you've mastered the basics and made many satisfying quilts. These accomplishments, wonderful as they are, seem only to deliver you to a nameless threshold. All you sense is that you're on the verge of the next step.

If this scenario is familiar and you think you're poised for that next step, then this book is an invitation. Consider adopting an independent approach to quiltmaking. Become the maker of your own quilts—yours, not mine, not someone else's.

Be forewarned. Striking out on your own, without comfort of pattern or instruction, can be lonely. The journey is neither smooth nor effortless. In the early stages, it can be perplexing and vexing. A host of anxieties frequently lurk in ambush, and demon voices emerge to exploit your uncertainty. If you're still intrigued and not alarmed by these revelations, then you're a candidate for independent work.

The Overview

The aim of this book is to prepare you for traveling the independent path. It reduces the apprehension by offering glimpses of the terrain, and it escorts you through some of the challenging regions. If independent quiltmaking interests you, then this book demonstrates that you have access to all you need for this expedition.

This book does not provide specific answers to every question, quandary, or neurotic moment. The result, otherwise, would be a fifty-pound book and certainly beyond my scope. It does, however, expose many common obstacles. And perhaps the simple disclosure that struggling is common, and not your private nightmare, may hearten you.

Working independently compels you to assume a creative stance. Many people recoil from the word "creativity." It's a beast they'd rather not encounter, at least not head on. So, within these pages, we expose the dragon and remove its fangs. Creativity and the creative process, commonly perceived as formidable and esoteric, are recognizable skills. They're inherent to all, including amateur quiltmakers.

Focused, individual work lends itself to exploring ideas. A natural outcome is developing ideas in a series. Working in a series is the best way to exercise creativity; each project is an extension and complement of the other.

Throughout the book, I refer to things that are of interest to me, like opera and art. And I'm enthusiastic about them. I don't play tennis or do motorcycle maintenance. If I did, I'd include these, too, probably with equal fervor. My personal interests have a bearing on my quiltmaking because they affect me, the quiltmaker. We aren't likely to share these same interests. Chances are, opera leaves you cold. (The percentages are decidedly in your favor.) But I know your life is full of its own charm and wonder and idiosyncrasies. These endow your personality, your quiltmaking, and your working rituals.

Despite all the suggestions and counsel, all you do depends on you—your individuality, your yearning. The overriding advice is this: Do and use whatever works best for you and ignore the rest.

The Pep Rally

Why Work Independently?

The desire to work independently comes from within. If you're not interested, no list of rapturous reasons can make you want to do this. But, if you happen to be on the verge of taking the step, or are simply curious, then it doesn't hurt to explore your inclination.

Personal Challenge and Reward

A basic human instinct compels us to challenge the status quo. Most pivotal points in human history are testaments to this observation, such as Gutenberg's press, the Polynesian voyages, and breaking the four-minute mile. Additionally, our long-standing identification with the underdog in almost any arena affirms this innate desire to challenge and succeed despite the odds.

Deep within us is the recognition that we reap life's greatest rewards when we reach beyond our perceived limitations, when we live fully from ourselves rather than from imposed formulas. *The Guinness Book of World Records*, as well as the long list of Nobel Prize winners, clearly attest to the wealth of ways to be challenged, to explore new territory, to be first.

If we aspire to evolve in our work, we must be willing to challenge and be challenged. Growth is impossible if we maintain the status quo (our own or someone else's), if we always do things the same way, without questioning, without exploring the simple pleasure of asking "What if ...?"

Skill and Attitude Improvement

Regardless of our starting point, the skills we bring to working independently will be improved. Motivated to move on to other projects in order to give substance to our ideas, we'll make more quilts. Skill improvement is not the result of frequent repetition alone. We may actually devise new methods in order to fulfill our vision.

Particularly noteworthy is how our attitude improves. In using our creativity, we experiment more and try new approaches. We innovate, through trial and error if need be. Because we accept that success builds on mistakes as well as victories, risk taking seems less threatening. We breach the onus of failure by trusting our ability to find a way out of the rough, by using more productively what we already know, including our intuition. We learn best through self-discovery. As we get better, our confidence prospers. "Why not?" becomes a valid working style.

Many people recoil from the word "creativity." It's a beast they'd rather not encounter. ... So, within these pages, we expose the dragon and remove its fangs.

Better Quilts

If we're grooving and improving, we can't help making better quilts, more personally authentic quilts, quilts that reflect our point of view. The independent quiltmaker will have difficulty making design choices based on someone else's criteria. Because personal growth is evolutionary, our quilts reflect and accommodate our new perspectives. The quilts evolve right along with us.

Personal Insight

In the absence of external guidelines, we learn to rely on ourselves. When invention and intuition plot the course of our work, they prosper and assume new credibility. Seen through an updated lens, the perspective for our work changes. Our self view is particularly transformed. We discover that we are bona fide quiltmakers and gain a powerful sense of our capabilities. If we're generous, we call this experience "revelation."

Fun and Satisfaction

People often struggle while having fun and seem undeterred by it. Marathon runners, crossword-puzzle enthusiasts, and chess players fall into this category. There are hikers who carry eighty pounds of gear on their backs, climb steep mountains, endure pain and blisters, and can't wait to do it again. It's the same with independent quiltmaking. Excitement exists alongside aggravation and struggle. For some odd reason, confounding ourselves with bits of fabric brings personal satisfaction. In stepping back from a finished quilt and seeing it as pleasing, our spirit soars. The toil it costs is obscured by the elation.

"... At Least We'd Have Been Somewhere"

At the beginning of the film, *Out of Africa*, Tanne is frustrated by the limitations of her social predicament. On impulse, she proposes to Baron Blixen and suggests they embark on adventures to lands unknown, issuing a litany of prospects to entice him. As she begins to run out of ideas, implying, too, that they might not even succeed at any of them, she concludes, "... at least we'd have been somewhere."

At this point, I, too, have run out of appeals for working on your own. I hope you begin this journey and profit from the experience. If for no other reason, at least you'd have been somewhere.

Why Work in a Series?

I've come to believe the best way to exercise our creativity is to work in a series—rather than playing the field of all possibilities. It focuses our energy; we improve at developing and advancing an idea. In the following studies, we resume the challenge by elaborating on it again. Through this reinforcement, we deepen our understanding of what we do in our style of quiltmaking. There are other reasons for working in a series.

Inspiration from the Masters

Working in a series is not a new idea. It's a fundamental approach in every field of art, as well as manufacturing and commerce. An example in the visual arts is the quilt-makers' current favorite, Claude Monet.

This French Impressionist painted water lilies, the Rouen Cathedral, and his gardens at Giverny numerous times—but not because he needed a supply of paintings for future museum collections. Rather, he was intrigued with the properties of natural light: reflection, refraction, absorption, and diffusion. His subjects were vehicles for interpreting this ephemeral play of light and for developing techniques for rendering what he saw. Monet created much of his work in a series, in pursuit of a greater understanding of light.

In a more contemporary mode, Andy Warhol, along with his paintings, is synonymous with the concept of the series. Recalling Warhol's Mao, Marilyn, and Campbell's® soup cans without this serial context is infeasible. The fact that we can bring forth in our minds, without hesitation, Warhol's images leaves nothing else to say. Their collective impact is visual testament to the series.

We don't need to look outside quiltmaking to find artists who work in a series: Nancy Crow, Michael James, Jan Myers-Newbury, Pauline Burbidge. Their names alone conjure images of exquisite, breathtaking quilts. They have transcended the medium, raising quilting into the realm of universal aesthetics. We are indebted to them for their contributions. They represent us well.

If great beauty and artistry distinguish the works of these artists, it's reasonable to assume there's something inherently valuable in working in a series. If for no other reason, just pretending to be right up there with their likes, plus the company of Piet Mondrian, Dale Chihuly, Georgia O'Keeffe, and other great serial artists, should be inspirational!

Impetus and Continuity

People often struggle while having fun and seem undeterred by it. It's the same with independent quiltmaking.

By working in a series, I create a hospitable climate for ideas. Either related ideas surge forth from disparate sources, or one idea germinates many. During this process, it's apparent that one quilt can't accommodate or be appropriate for all my ideas. A series is a natural conclusion.

The idea itself leads us on. The mystery of an idea is enticing. It tempts us to enter and explore unknown territory. We raise the stakes to see just how far we can chase a single, sometimes simple, concept. And all the while, this is play—despite the exasperating parts. The finished product, satisfactory as it may be, is visible confirmation of only one aspect of the idea. Inherent in every finished study is the impetus for the next one.

11

The Challenges of Transition

A beginning quiltmaker depends on patterns and instructions because there is learning to be done. Intermediate, advanced, and expert quiltmakers also rely on instructions when learning a new technique—it's part of any educative process, generally efficient and effective.

The difference between beginner and intermediate is the intermediate quiltmaker has enough experience to make a quilt from start to finish without coming to a technical dead end somewhere in the process. She feels comfortable and confident in her skills. Even when she encounters a bug or two, it's fixable and she still feels in command. This book is for that intermediate quiltmaker who is ready to make the transition into the world beyond instruction books.

An independent quiltmaker is one who seeks creative challenge and derives satisfaction from that effort. Usually, the challenge focuses on developing visual aspects of the quilt, rather than technique. Technique is a tool that contributes to producing desired, visual effects in quilts.

Independent quiltmaking is a departure from patterns and instructions. This transition is the first challenge in working independently: The quiltmaker must be prepared to retreat from the security of external instruction. There must be a willingness to think and act in a different, possibly new, way. If the new quilts are to be different from those of the past, then this can't be effectively achieved by doing things in the same manner.

If patterns and instructions are banished, then the quiltmaker must rely on other devices and schemes. This is the second challenge: The quiltmaker must be prepared to depend on internal skills and creativity. Relax. These don't need to be primed to full throttle at this very moment. There is great truth in the saying "Necessity is the mother of invention." You'll be impressed with how creative you can be when you have to. Whatever your opinion of your creativity, it's enough to get started. It's a skill. As with any other skill, it improves with use, and you'll be using it a lot.

These two transitions—surrendering instructions and relying on internal resources—can provoke anxiety. It's like being in a high-flying circus act. You're asked to release one trapeze, then grasp the second, which is momentarily out of sight. Scary? You bet. For some, this is a script of nightmarish proportions.

This is a good time to introduce the third challenge: The independent quiltmaker must be prepared to encounter taunting demon voices. For some people, these inner voices may be loud and clamorous; for others, it's just an occasional tweak of the ear. Your personality and experiences determine the strength or weakness of those voices.

Demon voices are unauthorized critics, and they sound like this: "You're going to use *your* creativity? Good luck! Where do you expect to

The independent quiltmaker must be prepared to encounter taunting demon voices.

find it? You haven't got any! Intermediate quiltmaker? Are you kidding? Remember that last binding, the one you cut too narrow, all forty feet worth? And binding's just the least of it. How about all those boxes full of unfinished projects? The real ugly ones you won't let anyone see. Give up instructions? Now there's a good one! You couldn't make a quilt *with* instructions. Bet you forgot about the 214 triangles you sewed together on the wrong edge. There is no way you can do this. You'll blow it for sure. Give it up before you really embarrass yourself."

Demon voices emerge when we're uncertain, lack confidence, and feel vulnerable. They're there when we take risks and stand on shaky ground, because the outcome is unknown. It's natural to want success. Fear is a projection of our imagination, a painful expectation of dread that hasn't yet happened.

I've heard my share of demon voices. In preparing this book, they came a-calling in droves. If you ever want to appraise your creativity, check out the clever tactics used by these voices to nail you. They are masters at ridicule. They expose your weaknesses and exploit your fears. Nothing is sacred. But consider that you had to have imagination and creativity to hear them. So, give yourself credit for producing these versatile creatures of mischief. Their rantings are interesting in a twisted way, and the more gullible the audience, the more riveting the details. Here's the good news: Over time, these voices lose their bluster and poison. Provided you're not taken in by their taunts, they soon lose interest.

If you're willing to give up the security of instruction, if you're willing to rely on your creativity, if you're willing to wrestle with demons, and if you're willing to risk all these things for an unknown outcome, then you've got enough courage for independent quiltmaking.

Working Independently
(the abridged version)

SKILLS YOU NEED:
Sewing Basics

**THINGS YOU NEED
TO SUPPORT YOUR EFFORT:**
Work Space
Time
Inspiration
Fabric & Tools

**CHARACTERISTICS YOU NEED
TO GET STARTED:**
Desire/Curiosity
Courage

**SKILLS YOU NEED OR CAN
DEVELOP AS YOU WORK:**
Color Idiom
Creativity
Perceptual Skills
Designing Skills

**CHARACTERISTICS YOU NEED
TO KEEP GOING:**
Desire/Curiosity
Courage
Resilience
Persistence

Tools for Independent Quiltmaking

Work-Friendly Environment

The most important thing we need for ourselves is a work-friendly environment. The components of this environment are space, time, and inspiration. These basic structures need to exist to support our efforts. However, for a host of reasons, there are gaps between the ideal and reality.

Work Space

Regardless of the size, it's important that the work space be carved out, designated, and reserved. Allocating space for ourselves is a signal to the outside world that we take our quiltmaking seriously. The work space may be an old table and orange crate in the corner of the laundry room or guest room, preferably without the guest. Whatever the arrangement, the work space should remain intact, undiminished, and be treated with respect. The larger the space, the greater the respect. I suspect the converse is also true: A small space will demand more than occasional defense of that turf.

Ideally, our work space is large enough to accommodate the following:

✔ **STORAGE.** Every quilt-related thing we have, need, and expect to acquire would have a home and be easily accessible. Maximum storage helps keep the actual working area clear of stuff that accumulates and breeds without encouragement.

✔ **MOVEMENT.** Creative quiltmaking, while having a sequence of sorts, tends to be chaotic in nature. There is an enormous amount of activity and manipulation of materials as ideas ignite, unfold, take off on tangents, get hung up, are reevaluated, switch gears, and take off again. Freeing ourselves from logistical frustrations allows a better flow of energy. Our work space needs to be large enough to accommodate both our ideas and the energy needed to bring those ideas to fruition.

✔ **DISPLAY.** Because independent quiltmaking is experimental, a lot of what we do are maybes: half-baked ideas that need further consideration. I have difficulty keeping all the maybes afloat in my head. Works in progress, works in suspension, works abandoned ("remember not to do this one again"), inspirational pictures, provocative assemblages—all require their rightful space. Front burner, back burner, whatever the designation, they need to be seen. That's the point: We can't make aesthetic visual choices about things we can't see.

Amateur-standing athletes practice hours each week. Aren't amateur-standing quiltmakers worthy of the same commitment?

✔ **PRIVACY.** There's a charmingly lilting song, "Im Chambre Separee," ("In a Private Room") from the Viennese operetta, *The Opera Ball*. The song extols the benefits and convenience of a private room, away from meddlesome crowds. Granted, the implied private activities of Viennese nightlife aren't quite the same as quiltmaking. Nonetheless, the basic premise is valid. It's advantageous to do what we do in a separate and removed space, away from distractions.

Creative quiltmaking requires concentration. Because we don't always know what we're doing, it is imperative to pay attention. Distractions, no matter how minor, can break that focus. Time is wasted in recovery, and some gossamer ideas are never recovered.

Privacy is also an advantage when we feel the urge to push ourselves, to try something unusual out of curiosity, for the sheer heck of it. If we blow it big-time and there are no witnesses, it's a relief knowing we were the only one privy to the misadventure.

Working independently is sometimes isolating. But this same isolation lets us talk to ourselves, laugh at ourselves, despair by ourselves, entertain ourselves. We can also play the kind of music or listen to books or lectures that other people think are corny or weird or boring. We can give them all the respect they deserve in our private space. In turn, they give us inspiration and/or pleasure, and there's nothing wrong with either of these supporting our creative working style.

Time

What I've said about space also applies to time. It, too, needs to be carved out, designated, and respected. The ideal is extended periods of uninterrupted time. Of all that we need for our work, enough time is probably the most difficult to acquire, especially with today's realities.

Time is critical because most of what we do is experimental. It takes time to play with an idea, to speculate, to test possibilities, then to modify them to suit. And this is when things are going well! There's a lot more messing about in many directions when testing sputters. Speculation consumes time.

Consider this: If you have children involved in sports, think of the time spent practicing. Daily sessions are mandatory to stay in the program. As the participants advance in skill and age, practice time expands to more hours per day. Amateur-standing athletes probably practice somewhere between ten and twenty hours each week. Aren't amateur-standing quiltmakers worthy of the same commitment?

I can feel the collective head nodding, but how to get those extra hours? Sorry, but I don't have secret solutions. Being super-organized is said to cut down on wasted time, which could be reapportioned. Increasing stretches of work time usually involves sacrifice. I say "no" more frequently to social commitments, clean the house less often (adopting a more cavalier attitude about dust), and eat more quick-prep meals than I care to admit. Unless you live alone, the proposal of somebody giving up something can be a prickly one.

Sweet Inspiration

There are no plans or patterns to follow for independent work. There are only ideas that originate in our subconscious. We make quilts by bringing these ideas to the conscious level, then organizing them, forging them into images from the materials at hand. Or better yet, cooperating with the spirit of the materials at hand.

Each of us has a dramatically different subconscious. It accommodates an incredible mixture of personal experiences produced through our senses, perceptions, misperceptions, and emotions. Without conscious effort, we're capable of increasing this reservoir; life happens, and impressions are registered, then stored.

Researchers theorize that only one percent of all information surfaces to the conscious level. I think it's less, but the argument is convincingly strong that we're capable of superstorage.

In superstorage, we preserve everything from the ridiculous to the sublime, from the petty to the potent, from the prosaic to the poetic. It's all in there. If computer technology teaches us "garbage in, garbage out," then it seems reasonable to assume "treasures in, treasures out" is also acceptable.

If the supposition is that our quilts have their origins in our subconscious and they reflect the contents of our subconscious, logic dictates that we take good care of the place. Beef it up. Fill it with extraordinarily potent material. Cue the dump truck!

Actively pursue inspirational material. Feed your head, nourish your heart and spirit. Where to go for this? "Follow your bliss," is Joseph Campbell's retort. In order to maximize an impression for abstract storage, the stimulus must first seize our attention, then persist in holding our interest. The easiest method of fulfilling this sequence is to access those things that have strong, inherent personal appeal. These, of course, will be different for each of us.

Do things that are pleasurable to the senses: listen to the birds sing or to the creek as it gurgles and slurps over rocks. Listen to the rain drum on the deck. Watch the ants scurry along the walkway, marvel at a spiderweb, watch how the wind ruffles the tall grass. Inhale deeply fresh herbs crushed between the fingers. Wear perfume. Smell the new day. Touch the grooves of tree bark, embrace a loved one, run your fingers over the surface of a quilt. Eat a piece of chocolate—savor it slowly. Drink fresh-squeezed orange juice, chew on a piece of jerky.

*Do things that
are pleasurable
to the senses:
listen to the
birds sing
or to the creek
as it gurgles
and slurps
over rocks.*

These are small activities with big returns. They are appealing and communicate to us without words. They produce sweet moments of pleasure, and our task is to pay attention to the enjoyment they bring. There are far too many things we do mechanically because we seem to need to. Because time is precious, we speed through the mundane and, perhaps in the process, sacrifice the gift of the ordinary.

Engage in activities that seem to be bigger than ourselves. Watch the sun set, sit at the top of the headlands and watch the waves roll in, visit the Grand Canyon, watch the Northern Lights. These are terrific visual images to store away. We needn't understand them or attempt to replicate them in future quilts. They are simply expansive, mysterious, and splendid, capable of transporting us outside and beyond ourselves.

Engage in activities that are out of the norm. If the norm is listening to Sinatra, try Bach or The Beatles for awhile. Sing along with great enthusiasm just for the sake of making a big noise. Dance around the room to Mariachi, Cajun, or Brazilian carnival music. Rent a foreign film for a different cultural perspective. Dine at a restaurant specializing in an ethnic food you've never tried— Ethiopian, Lebanese, Polish, Indonesian. Wake up that palate! Reread Emily Dickinson or Langston Hughes. Through books or museums, examine the masks of Papua New Guinea, the beaded necklaces of the Masai, the kimono and its accessories, Navajo sand paintings. Take a different route home; wear rhinestones to the market. Try anything you don't normally do. You certainly don't need to turn your life upside down in order to step outside of routine. A fresh new breeze to stir things up a bit is all that's needed.

Again, the point is to stimulate the senses in ways that produce experiences provocative enough to get imbedded in the subconscious. The more numerous the experiences and the wider the variety, the greater the capacity to make connections with the material at hand. When in the creative mode—whether we're sifting or dredging through our subconscious—there will be a richer vein to mine. There's really nowhere else to go for it.

In addition to increasing and improving the mind's inventory, there's another reason to indulge in new activities: to train yourself to shift from the standard ways of doing things. Look at it as stretching exercises that prepare you for taking more risks in your quiltmaking. It's a skill: the more you depart from the conventional, the easier it becomes.

Imagination

A friend of mine made an interesting observation, something I hadn't noticed before. She pointed out that most of my music collection wasn't in English. I wondered about this, then concluded I must have a preference for things I can't thoroughly understand. Perhaps, for me, the beauty of the music is enhanced by the enigma of unfamiliar musical patterns as well as foreign language. This condition of not knowing offers a great framework for filling in with one's imagination. Watching TV with the sound off would be a similar exercise.

Some people say they don't have an imagination. If you can fantasize about winning the lottery, building your ultimate studio, or traveling around the world and stopping at every fabric shop for souvenirs, then you've got imagination. And an exercised imagination is a dandy tool for making quilts.

Second to actually making quilts, collecting fabric sustains the creative process.

Tools

If you're a quiltmaker, I assume you have everything you need to make quilts. In my studio are the following items. They serve me well:

- Good lighting. Full-spectrum bulbs are indispensable, especially if you're a night worker, or the lighting in your work area is average. Standard lighting is substandard for work involving color.
- Sewing machine. A needle up/down function and either a built-in or attachable walking foot are essential options.
- Working surfaces. This includes a large rotary-cutting board. Keeping the surfaces clear is a Herculean task.
- Music source, with a broad range of music choices. The stereo comes with an off switch too.
- Display area (preferably vertical). I'm also content with the floor. When I'm moving pieces around, and quick switches are required, I find the floor a more agreeable surface. Unpinned things don't drop off and ruin the masterpiece. I suppose after all these years, I've grown accustomed to the odd perspective. Vertical expanses are great for keeping things up and visible for longer periods of time.
- Ironing board and steam iron, always up and ready to use. Contrary to all the advice out there, I like using steam to press. I've tried to use a dry iron, but I miss the sound and the heat quality of steam. This is a personal idiosyncrasy, not necessarily advice.
- Everything else, especially the smaller items are in multiples because they are easily lost. There are never too many pairs of scissors, thimbles, reading glasses, rotary cutters, calculators, seam rippers, et al. Does anyone have just one

bobbin? I refuse to spend time hunting for misplaced items when I have better things to do. If you pay even a passing homage to clutter, you might arrange for small items in multiples as well.

Fabric

Independent quiltmaking requires a fabric inventory. Bounty is necessary because no guidelines exist for the quilts about to be made. Independent, creative quiltmaking is based on speculation. We don't know the size, the colors, or the amounts. Inventory must be fairly large to accommodate what might be needed. Since ideas bubble up spontaneously, it's more convenient to commandeer fabric from an existing supply instead of dashing off to the fabric store when ideas flare. And since everything is subject to change, our fabric options need to be open and broad. To save our sanity, time, and fuel expenses, we need lots of choices at our fingertips.

At some stage, the quilt takes on a life of its own. If we're in dialogue with the quilt, then part of our responsibility is to listen to what it is saying. Generally, we'll see and hear that there's a problem with the way the fabrics or shapes are interacting. As with any relationship, neither denial nor coercion will bring about a satisfactory resolution. Change must take place. Switching and substituting may be required, and we can do this by re-auditioning fabric from our inventory. The greater the range of fabric, the greater the likelihood of success in fixing the problem.

Urging quilters to build and keep a fabric inventory seems an absurd bit of counsel. For goodness sake, we're notorious hoarders. We not only love fabric, we're nearly addicted to it. We have shelves, cabinets, boxes, closets, and garbage bags bulging and overflowing with the stuff. Our cars are equipped with homing devices that brake automatically for every fabric store. We buy it in person, we mail-order it, we trade it, and we pay money to enroll in fabric clubs. Worst of all, we covet our neighbors' fabric. We're shameless.

Of course, as far as inventory is concerned, lots of everything is best. But unless we're subsidized, this can strain the purse. Buy what you like—because you're going to make what you like—and use the material that appeals to you. When you're in the throes of designing and find yourself searching for plaids, you'll know immediately what's lacking if there are none. Fill in accordingly. Panic needn't set in if your inventory is thin or lopsided. Heck, Picasso spent years in his blue period. You could do the same.

Second to actually making quilts, collecting fabric sustains the creative process. The personal rapport we create with beautiful fabrics is the basis for interpreting them in our quilts.

Skills for Independent Quiltmaking

Technical Sewing

A working knowledge of the quilters' version of sewing basics is adequate for getting started in independent quiltmaking. These techniques include measuring, cutting, machine and hand stitching, pressing, and seam ripping. Should you determine that a particular virtuoso technique is required to pull off your quilt idea, then there's no way to get around learning it. But, knowing everything that could possibly be learned is not a prerequisite for starting.

Color Idiom

Pragmatic Color Theory, Speculations, and Heresies

The ability to create and use a color vocabulary is probably more useful than a studied knowledge of color systems. This observation does not dismiss the worthiness of studying color theories, which is, after all, an intellectual pursuit. Intellectual pursuits of any kind make us smarter and add to our quiltmaking resources. My statement merely encourages you to pursue beyond scholarship and create a color idiom that is yours.

Color theory is an orderly compilation of established, usually scientific observations. It's a convenient tool employed by painters, interior designers, florists, cake decorators, and other creative types. Conventional color theory is a tool—only one tool.

If established color theories are based on universal observations, it seems your personal observations about color could also serve as a basis for color theory of another kind. The measure of your theory's validity is its success; its application needs to fulfill and achieve a desired visual outcome. If it works and the user is satisfied, it's an effective color theory. Ideally, the working application of color is individualistic, pragmatic, and flexible. It needn't be dogmatic.

For several years now, I've worked on the Sisters Outdoor Quilt Show, held each July, in the little town of Sisters in central Oregon. Every year, we receive hundreds of quilts for display, with the number of quilts fast approaching the population of the town. I work as a member of the team that receives and documents these quilts. It's an annual treat to find myself smack in the middle of oceans of quilts. What is most refreshing (and rewarding) is discovering those quilts with unexpected pattern sequences and/or color combinations.

There's a mystique to these curious quilts, and I find myself wondering if the color choices were made out of necessity, out of creative intent, or unwittingly. They aren't applications or extensions of any conventional theory I know of. These quilts haunt me for days. Mostly, I cherish and honor the quiltmakers who simply did it their way. They have a special place in my heart, and their quilts are jewels in my personal cache of memorable quilts.

Fifteen different purple fabrics, each used once, is visually more scintillating than one purple fabric used fifteen times.

Unless we're making color (creating dye baths for fabric or mixing color pigments from tubes for surface application), color theory, as prescribed via the color wheel, has limited use in the quilt world. The standard color wheels, including linear charts, operate from an inventory of pure, fully saturated hues. In Quilt World, colors are available to us only as swatches of fabric. If a color is not in the store, on a bolt, or folded into fat quarters, it doesn't exist.

Most fabrics are prints. This means there are at least two hues or values interacting on the surface, affecting our perception of what that surface imparts as color. Additionally, there are the distracting graphic elements of pattern and picture. In all cases, prints will diminish, desaturate, or override the clarity of a particular color. While these may seem to be negative properties, it is these very characteristics that make prints attractive, serviceable, intriguing, and challenging as design tools.

Working with color families (versus the elusive, singular pure hue) may be more practical when designing with printed fabrics. Under these circumstances, it's easier to use a group of similar or approximate colors, such as a clutch of reds with some leaning toward rust, some toward orange, and some toward magenta. Grouping colors alleviates the stress of having to match them. There will never be the worry of running out of a particular fabric, because something close will suffice and usually proves better. Fifteen different purple fabrics, each used once, is visually more scintillating than one purple fabric used fifteen times.

Similarly, working with a color family provides a more ample field of play. Pinks and reds can cozy up to roses, fraternize with corals, then engage in a bit of friendly rowdiness with Halloween oranges. Taken altogether, their visual impact is greater than the sum of its parts. Think of it as an impressive musical chord. A chord is made up of individual notes, which when played simultaneously—particularly at poignant moments—can melt your heart, make your body tingle, or leave you breathless.

Within the world of color, personal perceptions of color are as valid as the dictates of conventional theory. Convention states that the warm family includes yellows, oranges, and reds, and the cool family includes greens, blues, and purples. Contradicting these accepted categories does not mean we're wrong. For neurological and psychological reasons, we each perceive colors differently. Our neurons and neuroses act as filters, affecting our color interpretations. For some, green may be perceived as warm, or red may have a cold connotation. Regardless of the reason, colors affect each of us differently. It may be better to appreciate color families that we perceive as warm and those that we perceive as cool.

By assigning sensate properties to colors, we secure them more vividly in our mind and imagination. Our access to color then is more sensual and experiential, less intellectual and abstract. If color manipulation extends from our personal, sensate responses—rather than from charts and textbooks—it's likely that the colors of our quilts will prove to be more vibrant, more personally resonant.

It also seems sufficient to recognize colors that are approximate complements. (A color's complement is its singular, direct opposite on the official color wheel.) For example, the customary complement of blue is orange. Approximate complements would be rust and mustard.

Our perceptions of color ... are influenced by a color's neighbors and surroundings.

It's helpful to remember that the essence of complementary colors is maximum visual intensity and impact through contrast. When used in combination, each complement simultaneously provokes the other to its utmost strength. Complementary contrast is a very powerful weapon, but high-voltage intensity may not be the visual intent of every quilt. By using approximate complements, it's possible to dilute the impact, yet still achieve and maintain a suitable and intended color dynamic. In practice, we modulate the intensity of the contrast by moving toward or away from the complement.

Relativity and proportion are aspects of color that are also useful in Quilt World and worthy of understanding.

RELATIVITY: Our perceptions of color do not occur in isolation. They are influenced by a color's neighbors and surroundings. Color is environmentally sensitive and interactive.

Value. A fabric of medium value no longer appears medium when flanked by fabric of dark value. The dark value pushes the medium value so it's perceived as lighter. When flanked by light-value fabric, a medium-value fabric is pushed in the opposite direction and perceived as darker. A color's value is always relative to its immediate surroundings.

When a very light color is adjacent to a very dark color, each simultaneously intensifies the value of the other. The white skull and crossbones against a black background is an illustration of the most intense light/dark contrast.

Hue. When a color is placed amid groupings of its own family—for example, orange with reds and pinks—it appears to assume some of the color properties of the family. It's as though each color is lending its color traits to the others. The eye relaxes and allows the blurring of color distinctions. Orange seems less orange when placed within its color family.

Conversely, when a color is situated amid groupings of a different family—for example, orange with turquoises and blues—its basic color is strengthened. Orange seems more orange. The eye is activated, becomes alert to the differences, and appears to reinforce them.

PROPORTION: Colors exist on a spectrum of frequencies, which means they have dimension and can be measured scientifically. Therefore, harmonic balance may be achieved among differing colors. As with a music chord, color harmony is a matter of mathematics, of measured increments and intervals. In both instances, however, mathematical formulas cannot be relied on to yield masterpieces in music and art. Formulas alone could not produce creations like those of Mozart or Bellini, of O'Keeffe or Gauguin. There must be a creative spirit governing what is optimally possible within the creation.

DELUXE COLOR: In quiltmaking, an obvious handicap is the lack of control over the availability of specific hues. Hand dyeing fabric is the only way to correct this. This limitation shouldn't be cause for lament, however, because color work in quiltmaking offers vast opportunities for subjective expression.

From the outset, all kinds of fabric may be selected from the wealth of bolts supplied by stores in the area, out of town, across the country, around the world. In vogue, too, are the sumptuous, intense, mouth-watering, hand-dyed hanks available from fabric-dyeing artists. Glorious, one-of-a-kind, uniquely personal, never-to-be-duplicated color palettes can be created from this wide array of choices.

From these palettes-of-plenty, quiltmakers can decide which colors (and by default, which value and brightness) to use. We control the specific size and shape of each color. We decide how much of a color to use. We choose exactly where and how often to place each color within a composition. We can change our minds about some or all of the above, then change them again and again and again. Quiltmakers are able to control the interactive dynamics of color because we exert control over those factors that create the dynamic: size, shape, placement, quantity, and proportion.

Modes of Thinking: Sibling Rivalry

Throughout the process of working independently, you will experience frustration and confusion. Sometimes these can be attributed to the left/right brain conflict and aren't a reflection of your ability. Understanding the conditions that spawn this bickering can help you distinguish between the two.

Since the late sixties, generalized theories on the dual nature of human thinking have entrenched themselves in the idiom of the day. Although there's consensus that our brain employs extremely complex systems of circuitry between different locales, we know and accept that the brain is divided into two hemispheres. The right and left sides process information in different ways. The left side specializes in verbal, analytical, sequential thinking; the right side favors the visual, perceptual, and associative.

An illustration of both modes of thinking is revealed by how we use the telephone directory. The left brain is at work when we look up a number in the white pages. Strict adherence to the alphabetical sequence is the only way to find any phone number in this section. That's one of the rules of the white pages. The left brain loves precise rules.

A similar search through the yellow pages proves fruitful if the category item is available within the community, for example, veterinarians, tow trucks, fabric stores. However, if the item is obscure, say, birdhouses, and a birdhouse heading is missing from the directory, the left brain, assuming failure, abdicates to the right. The strength of the right brain mode is its ability to make associations through imagery. It produces visual reckonings, which, in this case, is a plausible network of potential birdhouse sources, i.e., nurseries, garden shops, lawn-furnishing outlets, pet stores. The right brain loves speculation. It doesn't seem bothered by ambiguity.

The left brain loves precise rules.... The right brain loves speculation.

Quiltmaking uses both hemispheres, each assuming dominance at different stages of the process, that is, until one hemisphere disrupts the good plan by trying to assume dominance at inappropriate stages. Usually the culprit is the bossy left side. The situation then deteriorates into a classic power struggle. This clash of the hemispheres can leave the quiltmaker bewildered and in need of succor. A search for consolation, usually chocolate in nature, is paramount, although just about anything will do during harrowing battles.

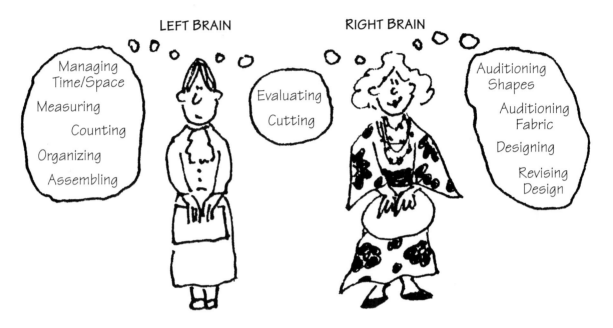

LEFT BRAIN — Managing Time/Space, Measuring, Counting, Organizing, Assembling

Evaluating, Cutting

RIGHT BRAIN — Auditioning Shapes, Auditioning Fabric, Designing, Revising Design

As a matter of routine, our reliance on the left brain is the basis for effectively getting through the day. Here, the processing of information is dedicated to facts and schedules: the gas gauge reads empty, so we stop to refuel; we check the due dates of our library books and bills; we make shopping lists. In most employment situations, successful evaluation is based on how systematically we function, how we adhere to the program and rules of the organization, and whether we complete assignments in a timely fashion. These and other survival tasks of contemporary life are the domain of the left brain.

Survival being at stake, it's no wonder the left brain assumes dominance in our daily routines and seems to relish the arrangement. At times, it acts the obnoxious know-it-all, even when it isn't and doesn't. Through habitual underutilization, the right brain retreats to its inferior position until summoned.

This portrayal is meant to invite sympathy for the right brain, because in situations of conflict, it's likely the right brain is struggling for position, while the left is trying to whip it into submission. This doesn't mean that the path of the right brain is always the glory road. It means there is an alternate way of processing information. The right brain should be encouraged to assume its natural dominance in certain situations, instead of retreating out of habit into the shadow of the left. Design is the domain of the right brain. Most of the work of independent quiltmaking occurs during the design phase. Make sure the right brain is in charge.

Perceptual Skills

As quiltmakers, we need to see basic edges, shapes, and lines. Knowing and understanding the properties of a given shape, whether a square, Buddha's smile, or an aspen leaf, implies an awareness of the shape's limitations as well as its potential. This kind of seeing goes beyond mere recognition and identification. What occurs is focused, immersed attention. Under scrutiny, the subject reveals itself to us, even though we do all the work. This revelation prepares us for manipulating design elements and is another handy tool for speculating about design options in quilts.

I recall in junior-high science, as preparation for the half-dreaded experiments of the fully dreaded lab classes, the first project involved observation. Our task was to look at a candle and flame, then list as many characteristics of both as we could see. Most of us stopped writing after about five or six items. When the smarter students moved into a second column of entries, we figured we needed to try harder. At the end of the session, the teacher disclosed it was possible to record more than 250 specific observations about the flame and candle. Even the brainy ones didn't get that many.

Gratefully, there was no grade, only a lesson to be learned. We needed to sharpen our ability to observe and see. Although we can get by quite nicely by attending to the general appearance of things, we need to see details in order to experiment. Observing details and coming to some preliminary understanding of them are prerequisites for conducting experiments. Regardless of any argument of aesthetics to the contrary, the making of art is, at its core, experimental. Whether in dance, music, sculpture, or poetry, the artist always says, "Let's try this."

Your perceptual skills can be improved, and the vehicles for doing this can be entertaining. It isn't necessary to limit your seeing to geometric or decorative forms.

Collectors have highly developed, discriminating eyes. They do research to acquire knowledge about their objects of desire, but they also train themselves to discern details. It matters little if one collects antique lace, rolling pins, or piggy banks. Whatever the object, the collector becomes its expert, cultivating skills through repeated acts of immersed attention, both visual and tactile. These skills are easily transferable and can be modified for looking at objects or shapes of any kind.

> *The paramount myth: Creativity is a rare, divine gift reserved for the anointed few.*

It is interesting to note that most visual artists are collectors to some degree. They surround themselves with interesting stuff—the curious, the provocative, the weird, the beautiful, the classic. Mary Engelbreit and Rachel Clark are collectors; Picasso was. Then, of course, there was Andy Warhol, The Consummate Collector of Stuff. His passion for acquisition was legendary and obsessive.

From our observations about physical, concrete things like shapes, fabric, or piggy banks, we abstract information. Abstracted information dwells in our subconscious—along with everything else we've accumulated there—where it patiently settles in dusty piles, awaiting opportunities to charge our imagination. And when our imaginations are charged, sparks fly. We've been known to call this phenomenon "creativity."

Creativity: Just Another Skill

When working independently, there are no patterns or instructions. Left to your own devices, you have no other choice but to tap into your creativity.

The Charmed-Life Myth

At this moment, from our varying perspectives, creativity, with its myriad associations, is seen as either intimidating or enthralling. The intimidation stems from myths perpetuated about creativity. The paramount myth: *Creativity is a rare, divine gift reserved for the anointed few.* The tandem myth: The vast, bungling majority of us are not, and never will be, among the anointed.

My guess is that we arrive at these conclusions through hopeless romanticism. First, we relentlessly associate creativity with raw genius, for example, Shakespeare, Mozart, Einstein, da Vinci, and others of their ilk. We admire them; we venerate them. Over the centuries, by perpetually comparing ourselves to the demigods, we see ourselves as pathetic mortals, forever doomed to mediocrity. Any desire, much less any active attempt, to voyage into the realm of the deified is viewed as futile and absurd. We are defeated by specious logic before we begin:

Mozart was creative.
I am not Mozart.
Therefore, I am not creative.

We may not be Leonardo da Vinci, but we each have our own particular view of the world. We may not be Bach, but we each have an authentic voice. We may not be Shakespeare, but we each have our own story to tell. Remembering this, we can more easily accept that there will always be luminaries who shine more brilliantly than the rest. This needn't preclude us lesser lights from twinkling in the same constellation.

As for Quilt World, the present reverberates with every stitch and patch that ever went before. It's impossible to sever our present knowledge from the past. It's equally difficult, and unnecessary, to divest ourselves of current influences. All segments of the arts—whether music, poetry, or dance—evolve from pre-existing conditions. We would have to live in a cave to be free of the influence.

Reverence for the tradition of quilts is shared by all who make them. Some quiltmakers reinvigorate the past; others venture into new territory. Whatever the course of interest, all expand and enrich the same collective tradition. Each day is a fresh moment in quilt history. Regardless of our quiltmaking status, amateur or professional, novice or experienced, each of us contributes to the legacy. When we seize this moment, we can choose either to donate carbon copies or tender offerings fashioned from our creative selves, however modest or spectacular.

"But I'm not creative!" Remember the mantra: "I have my own vision, I have my own voice." By substituting reality for the myth, we find that creativity is intelligence put to use in an original way. In essence, we gather information or apply what we already know to suit the needs of our situation.

In everyday circumstances, this creative activity occurs so spontaneously that we're unaware of it. For example, we find ourselves in a rain shower without rain gear. To get to the parking lot, we lift our pocketbook over our head and scramble to the car. Depending on the size of the pocketbook and the amount of rainfall, this may or may not be a total success, but we still behaved creatively.

If we've performed similarly at least once in our lifetime, we cannot say we aren't creative. Our creativity may be a little flabby, rusty, anemic, or timorous, but it keeps us alive. If we are alive and conscious, we have everything at our disposal to be creative.

The second myth about creativity: *Creative people always know exactly what they're doing.* They make no mistakes; everything is a masterpiece. In all the biographies and interviews I've read or heard, the only genius who could produce infallibly in every instance, without aesthetic revision, was Mozart. So if you're looking for inspiration, don't read about him. Instead, move to the lesser lights, such as Oscar Hammerstein II, Agnes De Mille, or Maurice Sendak. They describe, in one way or another, usually with uncanny directness, that sometimes they didn't have a clue. They simply worked hard at their craft. Some idea occurred, then they struggled, developed it, refined it, and hoped for the best.

Painter Willem de Kooning claimed, "Sure, sometimes I go through periods of real despair, look at my pictures, and say to myself 'What the hell am I doing?' " Writer Vladimir Nabokov said his pencils outlast their erasers. I love to read biographical sketches just to hear some esteemed person make these disclosures. What giddy relief! I always feel much better about my own fitful attempts.

After years of focused, committed, hard work, artists do go on to create with less blundering. Eventually, they approach their work with impenetrable awareness, having developed and refined those instincts that best foster the expression of their ideas. Their point of view and the ideas that extend from it are enmeshed with their execution. It's a fusion which, in retrospect, we label visionary. This fusion is illustrated in the choreography of Alvin Ailey, the glass sculpture of Dale Chihuly, the paintings of Georgia O'Keeffe, the puppets of Jim Henson. These are demonstrations of the concept and the delivery synthesized powerfully as one and the same.

The third myth about creativity: *Working creatively comes easily to those who are creative.* Again, from biographical accounts, there are streams of anecdotes about the creative struggle. They range from the monumental despair that sends some toppling over the edge of sanity, to the more typically neurotic skirmishes with self-doubt. During dry spells or weak moments, most creative people brim with assorted insecurities.

During dry spells or weak moments, most creative people brim with assorted insecurities.

Opera composer Giuseppe Verdi referred to his work as his agony. Fred Astaire said, "I like to dance, but it's such damned hard work." It was typical for Astaire to work intensively for four days in a row on two bars of music and, in exasperation, declare, "Why doesn't someone tell me that I cannot dance?"

Painter David Salle admits it's like beating his head against a brick wall. "When I work, I feel like I'm doing everything wrong. I feel that it can't be this hard for other people. I feel that everyone else has figured out a way to do it that allows him an effortless, charmed ride through life, while I have to stay in this horrible pit of a room, suffering. That's how it feels to me. And yet, I know that's not the way it appears to others."

Impressionist painter Paul Cezanne, in his seventies, acknowledged he was "progressing somewhat." Michaelangelo said, "If people knew how hard I have to work to gain my mastery, it wouldn't seem wonderful at all." Matisse said, "I wish my paintings to have the lightness and joyousness of springtime, which never lets anyone suspect the labor it has cost." Makes me want to hug them all, these kindred spirits.

For sheer entertainment, writers are the best at describing the terrors and tempests of the struggle known collectively as the blank page (blank canvas) syndrome. E. L. Doctorow claims that writing a novel is like driving cross-country totally at night. Mystery writer Sue Grafton says, "Each book feels impossible. Each time I write a book, I think I surely cannot do this. I have no skill. I have nothing left to say."

From what I gather, this angst afflicts everyone, regardless of the medium. Whether it's Karl Lagerfeld or Bill Blass preparing for the new fall fashions, George Balanchine or Agnes De Mille creating new ballets, or Oscar Hammerstein II or Alan Jay Lerner cementing lyrics to a new melody, dread, apprehension, and self-doubt are ever ready to disrupt the creative process.

Of course, when considering the works of the great, all we ever see, read, or hear are the triumphs. Who knows what disasters were tossed into fireplaces along the way.

I have dwelt on the twin tyrannies of fear and self-doubt in some detail because, of all the barriers to creativity, these take the lion's share. Personally, simply knowing that the greats and supergreats experience tumult acts as balm and fills me with resolve. If you have fallen for the myths of creativity, perhaps now your spirit will be more hopeful. It's this optimism that allows us to break the alliance with these myths and test our own wings.

Ode to the Lima Bean

Although usually oblique in nature, Zen masters offer advice that, once delivered, seems disarmingly obvious. Quoting a Zen master is where we begin: "To do a certain kind of thing, you have to be a certain kind of person." Translating this concept to our situation, we get: To make creative quilts, we need to be creative persons. Is this a breakthrough or what?

From gourmet chef to genetic biologist, the following traits are shared by many creative people in varying configurations. However, not all creative people have all these traits.

COURAGEOUS PATIENT FOCUSED
NONCONFORMING SELF-AWARE AWARE OF IMPULSE
OPEN-MINDED ATTENTIVE INDEPENDENT
PERCEPTIVE ENTHUSIASTIC
CURIOUS PERSISTENT ABLE TO HANDLE AMBIGUITY
HARD-WORKING FLEXIBLE
TRUSTING CONFIDENT RECEPTIVE SELF-REFERENT
PLAYFUL IMAGINATIVE OBSERVANT
ELABORATIVE SERENDIPITOUS INTUITIVE
EXPERIMENTAL RESILIENT

The following abilities also apply to creative people. Mastery isn't required.

TAKE BLIND LEAPS

BEAT YOUR HEAD AGAINST THE WALL

SPIN YOUR WHEELS

GO NOWHERE FAST

CHASE MUSES

HEAR THE MUSIC OF THE SPHERES

JUST SAY NO

STUMBLE WITH GRACE

WRESTLE WITH DEMONS

JUST SAY YES

GO WITH THE FLOW

STOP AND SMELL THE ROSES

GROPE IN THE DARK

CARPE DIEM

FLY BY THE SEAT OF YOUR PANTS

LAUGH AT YOURSELF

SENSE THE RIDICULOUS

EAT CROW

HAVE A NICE DAY

These lists appear to include everything except shadow boxing and masquerading as a lima bean. But we're open to them, aren't we, being creative and all…. Producing these lists does not produce a creative person. I know this. Nonetheless, I'm shifting emphasis by moving to an arena that puts these attributes in context. Having previously suggested that our creativity may be flabby, anemic, or rusty, identifying where and when these attributes occur proves more helpful than bustling about with a clipboard, rudely asking, "Well, are you, or aren't you?"

By the way, no one and nothing is preventing you from being or behaving as the above. Nothing, no one, at no time except you, right now. No one can create *your* quilts better than you. There is no one remotely qualified to do this. So if it applies, you'll need to transcend your self-induced inhibitions in order to get on with it. Who's gonna make your quilts if you don't?

Just as you can't swim by thinking, wondering, wishing, or fretting, you can't engage in creative work by just thinking about it. All things that require doing can't be done by proxy. So, paint your toenails blazing red for courage, suit up in something funky or fabulous, get wet, and plunge in up to your neck!

If personal daring is asking too much, here's another approach. Through modern, scientific instruments related to brain mapping, studies conclude that the mind can't distinguish between reality and the imagination. If you're shown a pineapple and are asked to look at it, then later, with the pineapple withdrawn, are asked to visualize a pineapple, the brain activity recorded for both exercises (seeing and imagining) is exactly the same. So, with science as your comrade, simply see yourself as creative. Fake it. Pretend. Your mind doesn't know the difference.

All creativity begins with an idea.

Creativity Considered

All creativity is fueled by passion. It is sustenance and motivation when all else abandons you. Creativity also demands your personal involvement, entirely. Without it, your quiltmaking is dictation, in the most profound sense of the word.

It's mind-boggling to consider that everything produced throughout the breadth and depth of all humankind was once someone's novel idea. From Camembert cheese to vinyl siding, from "Jingle Bells" to the Taj Mahal, these things didn't exist until after someone thought of them.

All creativity begins with an idea. In shepherding this idea to completion, something new is brought into being. This creation is a tangible version of the original idea. The idea and the tangible result are the first and last stages of the creative process, the beginning and the end.

Between these two stages is the vast middle section, which is fundamentally a field of countless deliberate decisions. Each single, organizing decision develops the original idea and advances the evolving form toward fulfillment. It's the accretion of these decisions that transforms a simple notion into a real monument, albeit a personal, modest one.

Observations on the Creative Process

The following is a discourse on the creative process. The phases and steps covered are sets of detailed observations. They don't necessarily occur in the sequence presented. Frequently, a few steps occur simultaneously.

Phase I: Idea Germination

Step One: Isolating One Idea

The first step to isolating an idea is acknowledging that you have one. Your idea is what you want to do or think you want to do. Your idea or intention may be described in terms that range from vague through general to specific.

General statements: I want to make a purple quilt. Or, it's about time I use this zebra fabric. Specific statement: I want to make a quilt that reminds me of tide pools at dawn. Vague statement: I think I know what I want to make, but I can't describe it in words. Here, all you have is an inkling, a propensity of feeling. Through experience, you know this, too, is a valid starting place. It's enough that your right brain signals the existence of an idea. Words aren't required for idea legitimacy.

At this point, your idea is still a fledgling thought, but it's an idea isolated from the other quilt fantasies roiling in your head. The purpose of Step One is to isolate your idea from all other distractions.

Because your isolated idea can capture your imagination and full awareness, it can also generate an energy field.

Step Two: Bringing Attention to Your Idea

By bringing attention to your idea, related strands of information mobilize and gather. Your idea acts as a magnet for everything you know, intuit, and experience about purple or tide pools. These sources can feel like palpable surges or wispy, vaporous allusions. Collectively, they become the energy field brought about by your attention. It supports your isolated idea.

Step Three: Being Available and Paying Attention

Serendipity is an intimate ally in this stage. Almost everything and everyone bears a fortuitous message about your idea—for example, supermarket conversations, the lyrics of popular songs, comic strips. All T-shirts, bumper stickers, and refrigerator magnets address you and make great sense. You see purple everywhere, and everything is a metaphor for tide pools. In this phase, you draw related information toward yourself and, in turn, are drawn toward the information you seek.

This convergence of information is not unlike what occurs in ordinary life. If your dryer dies in the middle of winter, suddenly you're fixated on all magazine ads and TV commercials about appliances. Every conversation includes your dryer mishap, and neighbors call to invite your wet laundry over for a spin.

When you shift your attention to something that concerns you, this attention creates an energy field that's relevant to the concern. These are gifts that support and enhance your life, including your creativity. Your task is to be available, pay attention, and take notes, literally.

Step Four: Taking Notes

Many of the ideas that occur throughout the creative process are mercurial. They're comparable to a mirage, appearing quickly, then vanishing. If they're not recorded immediately, they're gone. Give them form if you can. Write them down.

I wish someone had told me earlier that this was a legitimate step in quiltmaking. Although I was aware novelists notate dialogues, characterizations, and situations for future consideration, it never occurred to me to scribble my quilt ideas in a similar manner.

Many of my ideas flourish when I'm driving. Since the radio reception is lousy and my old car doesn't have an entertainment center, I ride in silence, driving the familiar country routes with detached attention. I believe this frame of mind, this half-consciousness steeped in quiet, is the precise breeding ground for allowing an idea to take shape. Steven Spielberg gets his ideas while driving, so I'm in good company.

Other activities yield similar results, such as bathing, riding the train, pulling weeds, taking walks. Any situation not requiring rapt concentration, but not so dull as to put you to sleep, is suitably effective. But the dream state of sleep is also a potent reservoir, so don't dismiss this activity too readily. As mentioned in Step Three, the convergence of energy flows from many sources. Be ready and grateful to receive it, regardless of the method or medium.

Step Five: Learning to Recognize an Idea

Beyond capturing content, there's another reason for taking notes: to sensitize yourself to an idea's occurrence, to learn its signs and symptoms. The experience of an idea is subtle and distinctive, but also fugitive and impossible to describe.

Consider your ideas as opportunities knocking at your door—or your head. If you haven't a clue what the knocking sounds like, then you won't be able to hear it when it happens.

Knowing what I know now, I'm positive that for most of my life I was numb to the occurrence of ideas. Lots of ideas may have made their debuts, but I never knew it.

Step Six: Restating Your Idea

Because the intervening steps put your idea in a larger context, a revision of how you see your idea may be appropriate. You may be considering an exaggeration of a characteristic or adding another component.

Reclarifying your idea can tell you what you're aiming for, at least at this moment, under current conditions. When you're stranded on a tangent, restating your idea will help you refocus.

Phase II: The Truth of the Matter

With the exception of note taking, the idea-germination phase involves activities of the mind. This next phase extends the play into the material world.

Step Seven: Material Gathering

Go to your fabric stash and begin auditioning and collecting those fabrics that are relevant to your idea. Muzzle that left brain and let the right brain do what it does best. Let it associate freely. Edit sparingly as you move along, and don't fret about the size of the emerging pile. Quantity is OK, even encouraged, but it is not the primary objective. Gather whatever it takes to fulfill your idea, and note that the assemblage is probably more than you'll use.

There's a tendency to get carried away by all the lovely fabric. This is a good sign. It means you are tuned in to the fabric. But should you find yourself drifting, take a deep breath and refocus.

On the other hand, if your fabric inventory is scant, you gain insight about your collection. Make amends whenever and however. In time, your inventory will better reflect the possibilities flourishing in your mind's eye. It's an unfair imposition on your creativity to want to make a dazzling purple quilt when there's only mauve and lavender smiling at you from your shelf.

Step Eight: Inviting Impulse and Intuition

Allow impulse to give expression to your idea and to guide your hand. This is intuition at work. Give it time to explore your inventory. Loosen up, relax, and let the process flow. Unless you've developed pyschokinesis, think of your hand as an intermediary between your intuition and the fabric. In this stage, you are the hired hand employed to move fabric from the general inventory to the working pile.

If you are using many fabrics to carry out your idea, this stage may require several hours, with recesses in between. Don't worry about the length of time spent here. Gag that accountant! Time spent here is an investment for later. A note of caution: If the left brain assumes dominance during this period, your working pile will look overcoordinated and predictable. Give your intuition a chance to strut its stuff, to lead you into a field of new possibilities.

Step Nine: Playing

Once you've finished collecting, play with your fabric. Move it around, build family arrays, discover curious combinations. Do it over, then again in new renditions and interpretations. Through these exercises, you transform the working pile into play-pile subsets.

To make the fabric easier to handle, fold all the pieces in a consistent way. While keeping the single fold prominent, overlay subsequent pieces in a row, with about an inch showing at the folds. This fanning out creates uncomplicated pattern or color runs and is a fair interpretation of how these particular fabrics react to each other in close proximity.

While you play with and manipulate your fabric, your right brain concurrently registers the visual results. It creates a memory bank of images and associations that you can draw from later. Hopefully, it will be there to rescue you from Mother Hubbard (bare cupboard) experiences.

Step Ten: Starting the Dialogue

You also recognize at this juncture that personal responses to your play piles are markedly stronger. They're no longer piles of strange fabric, and you're no longer the hired hand. You and the fabric grow in familiarity and establish rapport. It's this rapport and its sustaining dialogue that advance the creative process, keeping it relevant and consistent to the finish.

This development is a key step in the process because it's the fabric that carries out the tall order of expressing your idea. Knowing your fabric allows you to coax the necessary performance from it. The rapport also allows the spirit of the fabric to guide you toward the unexpected.

Step Eleven: Distinguishing the Fabric

Through rapport, you detect that some play piles affect you more favorably than others. They earn your attention. They have the right tone, the right feel, the right expression. They're better than the rest. Basic as it seems, this realization is a genuine discovery, for now you're able to loosely organize your material.

I find that a minimum of three general organizing categories is typical: the prima donnas, the supporting roles, and the chorus. Each category has its part to play, and each must relate to the others. Both singularly and collectively, these organizing categories contribute to the integrated whole.

I retain a separate and physically remote pile for the outcasts and misfits. This pile is the first line of substitution when I'm stuck and the primary categories have failed. When the outcasts fail, I re-audition the general inventory. It happens—and not infrequently.

Step Twelve: Recognizing What's Going On

Although the basis for the categories may seem subjective, by playing and auditioning, you begin to understand the truth about your fabrics. You see how they respond to each other, where their flexibilities lie, the strengths of some, the weaknesses of others. By building on this knowledge, you learn what's going on with your players. Although you may not always know what you're doing, you groom your ability to recognize what's going on with the material as it exists, as it's presented to you.

Phase III: Just Do It

I ignore the side trip of technically preparing fabric, for it depends on what you're planning to do. For some, this means making new fabric, as in strip piecing into preliminary sheets. For others, it means cutting pieces into required shapes—triangles, petals, body parts. Since most of my ideas are vague impressions and I design as I go, it's pointless to cut everything in advance. When fabric requirements are ambiguous, cutting several pieces from an assortment of working fabrics offers enough breadth to get started. As the composition evolves and imparts more visual cues, fabric demands become clearer and more specific.

It's my old buddy, the blank-page syndrome, making its shadowy appearance. Suddenly, tidying the studio becomes the most important task in my life.

Step Thirteen: Starting

I laugh when I get to this stage because I know what needs to happen, but inevitably there's hesitation. It's my old buddy, the blank-page/blank-canvas syndrome, making its shadowy appearance. Suddenly, tidying the studio becomes the most important task in my life. Half the time, I succumb. I clean up and try to rationalize that this really is a preparatory, space-making ritual. But I know I'm kidding myself with anxiety-aversion tactics. As long as I'm aware of playing the silly game, the worst consequence is that I waste a little time.

So begin. Start somewhere, anywhere. Take a handful of pieces, move them around, and set them in place on the design surface. If it doesn't feel right after a few moves, you'll know it. Begin again, over and over as needed. Don't fight the process, don't lament the jerkiness or arbitrariness of your moves, and above all, don't force anything to happen. The spirit of this activity is doodling.

Step Fourteen: Experimentation

When you're stuck, experiment. Experimentation is the reprieve from the dormancy/vitality impasse, that is, when the vitality of your idea is thwarted by the temporary dormancy of your ability. When you operate in a visual vacuum, where there's nothing yet established to offer clues, it's awkward and you'll feel inept. If you have any desire to get on with it, experiment. Without clues, you're compelled to do so. Yes indeed, this is experimentation, the trial-and-error variety. Say to yourself, "Let's try this." Or, "What if …."

Experimenting in a visual vacuum is demanding and exhausting. This is the toughest step you'll encounter, because everything is sketchy and skeletal. Since most of the visualizing takes place in the imagination, your mind may blow a few fuses. Patience and your best, undisturbed concentration are needed, so don't plan to do this on the day of your baby-sitting exchange. Spend as much time here as necessary, because it's on this locus that the quilt evolves.

Experimenting is also an opportunity to temporarily forget what you know. Because the mind is cluttered with conventional devices, it's necessary to suspend the temptation to use tired, conventional, ready-made, shortcut solutions.

Step Fifteen: Adjusting to New Stimuli

Whatever you're doing is a new perspective for your eyeballs. Since it's new, and therefore unfamiliar, your eyes and brain need time to assimilate the stimulus, then come to some understanding about it. You're not striving for penetrating comprehension here, just a simple visual reckoning.

Don't expect anything visually thrilling; this is a preliminary step, with only a fraction of the work available to the eye. Perhaps your work looks trifling; you feel disappointed. If you don't anticipate this initial disappointment, your self-doubt finds a toehold. Here, the hard job is deflecting the demon voices: "This is trite…. This is going nowhere…. After two hours of torture, this is the best you can do?"

After organizing a few pieces to your lukewarm satisfaction, leave it and go away. Allow this little starter sprout to take hold, to germinate, to come into its own.

As this is another germination phase, the activities previously mentioned also apply: be available and pay attention. Ditto for all germination periods whenever they occur.

Step Sixteen: Evaluation

Return with fresh eyes and determine what you've got. Evaluate it against what's possible in light of your idea or intention. If you can say, "It doesn't look like much, but it could work," that's an honest, descriptive comment. It's a start, and you've got a keeper. You don't need to fuss or push for more right now.

You don't have to like what you see either. Liking or not liking has nothing to do with what you're doing at this stage. As long as it's relevant to your idea and it appears to have some promise, it's fine. Besides, there's not enough substance here to support infatuation, so don't allow emotions or inner critics to interfere with what you're doing. Savor and love it later.

Step Seventeen: Adding Elements and More Evaluation

Add to what you have and look at it; evaluate it. From this step onward, whatever you do either works or doesn't. Not a profound statement, but being mindful of it prevents two major pitfalls: 1) You can't force it to work (coercion), and 2) You can't pretend that it works when it doesn't (denial).

… don't allow emotions or inner critics to interfere with what you're doing.

Without exception, every quilt disaster is attributed to one of these two pitfalls. If your evaluation is either misrepresented or ignored, you won't be able to create the result you want. Your work is in peril. I've been there, done it. In retrospect, I know exactly where and when I might have salvaged the monster, but I chose to ignore or misrepresent the obvious. Or chose not to fix it because the task was bothersome. Or hoped it would fix itself. Or fooled myself into thinking that it wasn't that bad anyway.

So ask yourself, "Does this work?" If it does, then carry on. If it doesn't, and your "gut" knows it, then you need to adjust or change something.

Even when you're improving something, making changes and adjustments is inconvenient. This is one of those immutable laws. It's true for everyone, every time: Fixing something is a necessary hassle. Postponement of the inevitable won't eliminate the problem or make corrections any easier. Whine if you must, but steel yourself to fix it now.

Step Eighteen: The Working Dialogue

Here, the hard job is deflecting the demon voices …

When framing the question, "Does this work?" consider the following factors: What have I got? What did I just do? Do they relate to each other? Do they relate to my idea? Address these factors each time, with every move and/or change. Taken together, this sequence is your working dialogue.

On occasion, you may intentionally suspend answers because a more complex motif isn't developed enough, but the questions still need to be asked, and answers provided eventually.

The questions are based on perceptions, and your answers are based on sensations. These sensations are intuitive, sometimes visceral, responses to the visual data. Pay attention to the details and listen carefully to how you're responding. If you have a hunch, it's likely to be your subconscious sending you a message.

This little sequence of "Does this work?" is the working dialogue. The working dialogue directs your entire production, so understanding it is crucial. It's the linchpin to the whole creative process. Until you get to the end and stop, you engage in this working dialogue repeatedly, continuously. Even if you develop an abridged version, the dialogue is enforced all the way through to the finish. Approaching the dialogue with honesty, you know what you're working with, and you know where the work is going.

Step Nineteen: The Working Continuum

Anytime you take action, whether it's progressive or remedial, you restructure and redesign your quilt. Throughout the entire process, your production is regulated by a series of perceptions and responses. The process is based on the ability to observe the consequences of what's being done and how each step connects with what's there. In this way, all your actions are cumulative, a summation of purposeful, serial acts. They aren't routine, arbitrary, or frivolous.

Because each act retains what's gone before—with reference to what's to come—each act is instrumental to the other. As these interact and mutually modify one another, you create a relational consistency to your work.

Phase IV: Internal Workings

Step Twenty: Learning As You Go

You might recognize what you're working with and know where your work is going, but you might not always know what you're doing. In truth, throughout much of the process, you'll learn as you go. It's a continuous cycle of speculation, tests of visual congruity, and decision making.

Blunders will be made along the way. You can't invent new dance steps without stumbling. You can't tackle new slopes without an occasional spill. So, you can't improvise your way through a new quilt without goofing up somewhere, sometime. It's intrinsic to the process.

By performing only the familiar, you won't make mistakes. This is a guarantee. Redundant pursuit of the familiar immunizes you from risk, but it also nullifies experimentation, which is at the core of creative endeavor.

Step Twenty-one: Yielding to the Process

Built into learning as you go is the excitement of having blunders reveal something unintended. Before you foreclose on what appears to be a dreadful mistake, take a second look. Depending on the vantage point, blunders can be seen as disasters, mistakes, accidents, or incidents. Notice how the nasty negativity drains as we advance through the list.

This exercise practices a very special maneuver: You learn to yield to the creative process. You broaden your view of the material, your evaluative skills, and your design options. Once you shift your perspective and yield to the process, you can better develop the accidental or incidental to suit your needs.

Built into learning as you go is the excitement of having blunders reveal something unintended.

Seeing only a full-blown disaster will put you on the defensive and induce tunnel vision. Because all you see is the disaster, you want it to go away. With tunnel vision, you eliminate an unplanned option before you even recognize it as such.

Keep a flexible attitude and be willing to make shifts in perspectives. Who knows, this may be divine inspiration. Pay attention.

One way to increase your ability to make shifts in perspectives is to develop a sense of humor. In comedy and cartoons, ordinary situations are still ordinary situations, but they're funny because certain details are brought into relief and viewed in surprising and unexpected ways.

Then again, the blunder may very well be pure calamity, as aptly seen the first time around. This happens too. It keeps you humble.

Step Twenty-two: Experience and Assimilation

There's a sign in my room that reads: "Good judgment comes from experience. Experience comes from bad judgment." Experimenting, allowing mistakes, making the necessary adjustments, then learning from it all is the course of experience.

Somewhere along the learning curve, experience also teaches that learning needn't be acquired solely through trial and error. Over time, experience prepares you to anticipate and avoid errors. You develop early-warning signals that detect your potential waywardness. This is your intuition at work. The more you create, the greater the likelihood of developing a keen partnership with your intuition, which also enhances your decision-making ability.

Step Twenty-three: Operating from the Center

In addition to a general passion for quiltmaking and the desire to see the end result of your effort, the force that nurtures the work through to completion comes from your center, a place within yourself.

Professionals in the performing arts and sports have a center from which they perform. It is out of this still place that their appropriate action comes. They don't burst indiscriminately, hell-bent-for-glory, into the stream of activity. Observe them. Immediately prior to issuing the first note or taking the first step, they prepare by coming fully into themselves. It's this composure, a composing of oneself in the context of the situation, that is their strength. It's this knowing and trusting from the center that brings conviction to their performance.

High-octane willpower and grit-your-teeth determination do not enhance your capacity during the more challenging aspects of the creative process. Instead, they produce tension, which greatly interferes with your work. They sap, not enhance, your energy. Know, regain, and hold your center, then operate from there.

Step Twenty-four: Terra Incognita

You won't be delivered from ambiguity. The creative process is fraught with it. With experience, you get better at handling ambiguity, but it never goes away. This is because the process requires that you make forays into the unfamiliar. They may be bold leaps or baby steps, but always into a strange land.

Whenever you journey beyond your imagined boundaries and stray outside your cozy patches of comfort, familiar landscapes disappear, and you enter unknown territory. There are no maps, no worn paths, no guidebooks to aid you in adapting to sometimes inhospitable terrain. When you're alone in the heart of darkness—and in desperate moments that's what it seems like—you lose orientation.

Press on and fear not—it's only a quilt! Even if your creation falters and you see buzzards circling, no one's going to burn you at the stake or banish you to the dungeon. The worst that can happen is you waste a bunch of fabric. So, keep your perspective, maintain your sense of humor, and try again. This is exploration. You're discovering unknown worlds and learning a lot about yourself in the process. This is the fun part. It's also heroic, this lonely wandering with only vague, internal references and invisible support systems.

Press on and fear not—it's only a quilt! Even if your creation falters and you see buzzards circling, no one's going to burn you at the stake or banish you to the dungeon.

Step Twenty-five: Confusion

Confusion emerges from a conflict of equally worthy aspirations. This conflict can keep you in a jam, not knowing which way to go. When more than one option can fulfill your intention satisfactorily, and you can't decide which to choose, this is stalemate. Languishing here is uncomfortable, and you beg for a redemptive miracle or a glimmer of inspiration, at the very least.

Sometimes you get the nod from the muses and you're led blissfully into the next step. But usually you don't get divine intervention, so the decision making is all yours. After groaning, you choose—eventually. You make the decision, because there's no other way out of the dilemma. The solution sounds simple, but it's hardly ever easy.

Step Twenty-six: Being Stuck

Being stuck is part of the process too. It means you care about what you're doing. If you don't care, then anything you do to get to the end is good enough. When you care, you know it's necessary for your maneuvers to fulfill your idea. If they don't work, you're paying attention. You're attentive enough to know this current move is inappropriate at this particular place, in this particular way. Sometimes even the second, third, tenth attempt won't work either. But being really stuck is not even having a clue about what the next attempt should be.

Unusual as this sounds, over time, being stuck is no longer formidable. Although it doesn't become gleefully anticipated, you realize your perception of it changes. You understand that barriers transform into stepping-stones, even without the fairy godmother. Eventually, with a string of little successes bolstering your confidence, you acknowledge that being stuck is a preliminary position. It's a preparatory state for breakthrough. Unless you're stuck and backed into a corner, you can't experience the exhilaration and surprise breakthrough brings.

Breakthroughs are not guaranteed. Persisting through the struggle, no matter how exasperating, boring, or awkward, is one way. Patience with the process is another. Patience also includes temporarily leaving it alone, not doing anything to confuse you further, allowing new energy to gather around it. When all else fails, exhorting the gods again is a valid option.

Step Twenty-seven: The Epiphany

This is the groovy part of creativity, the part that gets the hype and press coverage. An epiphany is a spontaneous visit of the muses. They come to frolic in your idea's playground. They come from out of the blue, perhaps as result of your pleading or deal making. But if you aren't there tilling the field and if you aren't paying attention, the key moment can be missed. So, work hard, pay attention, and keep a red carpet handy.

MUSE COURTESY #1: For goodness sake, don't ignore the muses. Their appearances are rare enough, so don't blow it by being so absorbed in your own agenda that you miss the glorious, spontaneous moment.

MUSE COURTESY #2: Let the muses do whatever they want. Concede immediately that whatever they do is just fine. Changes? Detours? New directions? Scrap the whole thing and begin something else entirely? Not a problem.

MUSE COURTESY #3: Thank them for the honor of their visit.

Step Twenty-eight: Running on Empty

While driving earlier this spring, I wondered, "Why is this car so hot?" When I noticed the heater was on, I turned it off.

Creative quiltmaking is fun, but demanding work. As part of the challenge, you up the ante, turn up the heat. This works well some of the time, but occasionally, you've simply got to turn the heat off. Even Picasso admitted: "You can't be a sorcerer every day."

In fact, sometimes it's a good idea to shut down altogether. Give yourself and your quiltmaking a rest. Some days you're just not up to it, not any of it. Nothing works. You're spinning your wheels and feeling ambivalent. Before you burn out completely and find yourself in a little heap of ashes, take a break. Abandon it for awhile. Liberate yourself. Take a vacation from quiltmaking. Refresh yourself by doing something entirely different. Go to the zoo, visit another town, fly to Portugal. Upon your return, a fresh perspective will provide clarity about what you're doing.

If your best quiltmaking comes from yourself, then you can't run on empty. Get refreshed, recharged. Recreate.

... the impulse for the "next one" is infused in the present. Built into the creative process is its own self-perpetuating momentum.

Phase V: Assimilation and Momentum

Step Twenty-nine: Personal Reinvention

Each step, whether successful or not, teaches you something about the next, and each breakthrough adds to your body of knowledge. Because the knowledge is hard-won, you internalize what you've learned, and gradually it becomes a part of you. This is assimilation. Over time, it accrues and you become more fluent in using what you've learned. It also transforms you. Through assimilation, you reinvent yourself, and this new, more competent self embarks on the adventure, outfitted with resources and expanded abilities.

Step Thirty: The Power of the Process

The power of creativity is the process itself, all of it. It's the idea besotted with curiosity. It's the doing and the making. It's entertaining the struggle and delighting in the surprise of breakthrough. It's the adventure of exploration and discovery. It's creativity for its own sake, for the pleasure and satisfaction of doing it—regularly, daily, every fortunate moment.

A rosy retirement is never part of the future fantasy for writers, musicians, painters, quilters, because the impulse for the "next one" is infused in the present. Built into the creative process is its own self-perpetuating momentum. There's nowhere to stop. Vacations and rest places occur, but for the sole purpose of refreshment, for the improved capacity to get on with it once it's revisited.

Step Thirty-one: Self-Appraisal

Because you care about what you do, you will engage in self-appraisal. This activity is not to be confused with neurotic bouts of self-torture—beating up on yourself for not being perfect. There's nothing competitive or comparative here. Self-appraisal involves introspection. It's an assessment of some basic truths about how you approach your work, then acknowledging what's revealed.

Here are some typical questions: Are you honest with yourself? Is the work created for you, or are you trying to make an impression? Are you trying too hard, so your work looks contrived? How focused or dedicated are you? What is your vision? How much of your vision comes through in your work? What are you good at? Is what you're good at integrated into your vision?

Answering these sorts of questions with integrity is a valuable exercise. Think of this information as a compass reading: it helps keep you and your work on course. Although self-knowledge is always an asset and never a hindrance, don't get too fixated on this exercise. A few times a year is more than enough.

There's also a kind of serenity that accompanies the acceptance of truth. You're less likely to be swayed by the distractions of Quilt World, titillating though they may be. As with life in general, external circumstances have little to do with your essence, from where your best work flourishes.

Step Thirty-two: The Key

Despite all the suggestions and guidelines, all you do depends on you—your individuality, your experiences, your yearnings. Your journey of exploration and experimentation makes you the expert of your own creative process and style. In the end, that's all that matters. Take time to discover what comes naturally, and build on that strength. Derive enjoyment from what you do, and ensure that it's a sustained condition in your life by giving it priority. Be generous and share what you have and know. Whether you assent or not, you are muse to someone else.

Take time to discover what comes naturally, and build on that strength.

Working in a Series

A series is a body of work connected by a common idea. Producing a series is a natural consequence of how we work. The series emerges in two ways. The first way is a by-product of the creative process. When working creatively, related ideas surface to support our effort. (Remember the right brain? It's there, bombarding us with associated ideas.) Since all our ideas can't be incorporated into one quilt, a series is a solution. Managing the ripple effect of ideas produces a series.

The second way is more deliberate. Instead of accommodating an excess of ideas, we decide to explore the possibilities of a single idea. In this approach, a subject or idea is consciously studied, and compositions are created. These studies embody the results of our particular investigations, explorations, or experimentations.

Whether the series is the result of associated ideas or an isolated idea, it all starts with just one idea. In general, a series is a set of variations on a given idea. Jazz provides a good example of the use of variation. In jazz, improvisations, or variations, are made upon the melodic structure of a song. None of the variations are note-for-note versions of the original piece. Instead, they're innovations, new interpretations of the familiar. Although the bars and measures usually remain intact, the notes within them are modified. They are compressed, reconfigured, exaggerated, eliminated, and given character and vitality. The melody remains as a subtly recurring, central motif.

Initiating a series needn't be an intimidating prospect. It doesn't require much—just one idea. And the one idea generates its own momentum, with or without prodding.

Inspiration for a series can come from any source. It can be literal or metaphorical, such as trees (Erika Carter), the garden (Jane A. Sassaman), or mazes (Ellen Oppenheimer). It can be abstract or conceptual, such as passion (Nancy Crow), overlay (Ruth Garrison), or expectations (Sue Benner). Any idea can work.

Whatever you're doing right now can launch your series. Let's say you're making a Christmas quilt. By extending the idea, you could embark on a series of holiday quilts. There's Halloween, Valentine's Day, Aloha Week, Summer Solstice. If you're making a traditional Double Wedding Ring quilt, you might next consider very untraditional rings, such as circus rings with high-flying, uproarious motifs, then ethnic rings, calling upon the richness of various cultural influences.

Working in a series shouldn't impose upon your current effort. You're likely to be more productive, more committed, and more sincere if your series develops from your natural inclination and interest. Whether bathrobes or ballet dancers, calla lilies or the triumph of virtues, all subjects are valid.

If you've got an idea, then make that quilt. If you're working independently, it's likely another interpretation will occur to you without much inducement. That will be your second study in the series. It continues this way until you decide the idea has run its course.

So, if you and your idea are ready, skip down to "Study Hints" below. On the other hand, if you're tempted by the invitation to work in a series, but nothing comes to mind, then the series format presented in this book could be helpful. This series was developed specifically to make it easy to warm to the task. It is by no means the only way to tackle the subject.

The Series in This Book

Five simple quilt-block patterns form the basis for five distinct series in this book. Each block pattern is the nexus for the series: it generates a traditional study, then other variations follow.

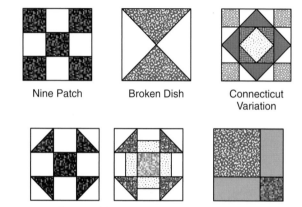

Nine Patch Broken Dish Connecticut Variation

Shoo Fly/Churn Dash Odd Couple

I selected patterns from some of the simplest blocks available. I chose them for two reasons. First, they were easy units to construct. I didn't have to agonize over the technical aspects of making them. With the mechanics under control, I could steep myself in the exploratory and design aspects of the studies. Second, they were familiar. Throughout the design, redesign, and assembly stages, remembering the sequence didn't demand the use of intricate blueprints. The simplicity and familiarity of the blocks also served as psychological support. Even though I didn't always know how I was going to use this structure, at least there was security in the jumping-off place. For a variation to occur, I knew the leap needn't be quantum.

I developed a series of quilt studies for each block. Each quilt is a compositional study, a visual variation, developed around the structure of the block. In some instances, the structure of the block contributes significantly to the quilt design. This is particularly true of the traditional examples. In other studies, the overall composition prevails over structure to such an extent that the block pattern is imperceptible.

In the most general terms, the mandala is a revered, spiritually symbolic illustration. Although present throughout many cultures, revealing the cultural, social, and psychological inflections of each, there are some fundamental characteristics common to most mandalas. Mandalas are almost always concentric, and there is reference to the four basic elements (earth, wind, fire, and water) or directions (north, south, east, and west). Visual balance or symmetry is also a prominent feature. Because of the mandala's application, balance and concentricity are not aesthetic devices, but rather demonstrations of a philosophic ideal.

In those cultures where mandalas are still used, not just viewed as artifacts, they are vehicles of spiritual practice. They are sources of meditation or instruments of healing. Since the integration of the mind/body/spirit is still an intact concept in these same cultures, therapeutic practice is holistic, encompassing all aspects of the human condition.

The Mandala series (on pages 77, 84, 86, 87, and 89) is a separate compilation of studies gleaned from the original block studies. It is a conceptual series, where the idea of the mandala and its visual interpretation takes precedence over the familiar pattern of the blocks. The block construction is simply a means of assembly.

Getting Started

Review the gallery of quilts and find something that suits your fancy. Whatever you select, I strongly suggest that you make a traditional version first, even if you've made twenty of them in the past. (The versions in this book are not the only traditional treatments around. If you've a supply of quilt books, you may want to do comparative research.)

The purpose of producing a traditional version first is to focus attention on what you're developing *now*. You're making the idea current and framing it within a fresh context. You're also establishing a point of reference. Subsequent studies will refer to this idea or form, even if remotely.

So, make the traditional quilt and take mental notes about what you're thinking as you make it. It's probable that one gnawing reaction will be monotony. The simple repeat can get downright tedious. At the same time, because you're bored, you're likely to devise a jillion ways of redesigning this insufferably simple pattern just to keep yourself entertained. Well, this is it! You've stumbled upon the basic tenet of working in a series: Through your own imaginative devices, regardless of the stimulus, you spin off new variations.

OK, even if you recognize this devious ruse for developing a series from scratch, it's still advantageous to make a traditional version first. Consider the traditional study as an opportunity for research and development. That sounds official enough. So, humor me: finish the traditional quilt top, and meanwhile, cultivate design ideas for future studies.

By the way, color switching from one study to another doesn't count as a variation. For example, making a Nine Patch in Christmas prints, then substituting Halloween and Easter prints in exactly the same way for studies #2 and #3 does not constitute variations. This would be like singing "Camptown Races" in the key of C, then singing it in the keys of F and G the same way, all the way through. Remember the jazz illustration: You need to improvise on "Camptown Races," not just repeat it note for note in a different key.

Study Hints

Keep your studies small. It's more practical in terms of time and materials. Don't tax yourself unnecessarily with a king-size quilt just to bring one modest study to light. Working in a series is propelled by a wild hankering to make the next one. So, keep each project small—at least finish the top—and move on with gusto.

Think of your quilt as a very large block and design it accordingly. I suggest this because most intermediate quiltmakers are fantastic at designing 9" or 12" blocks. Their use of color is sophisticated, and the elements hum along beautifully. So, the challenge now is to shift to a larger canvas. Instead of a 12" block, think of your quilt as a 40" or 60" block. It's the same approach, only bigger and with more pieces.

Your imagination is a powerful tool. At times, its strength may interfere with your work. While working on a study, somewhere around two-thirds through, your mind may project its completion. In your mind's eye, you've finished the study and resolved the original challenge. Your mind also has in reserve brilliant ideas agitating for the next study. So, you may find yourself wrestling with the dilemma of going with the flow versus completion.

There are arguments both for and against each horn of this dilemma. If you're seized by that wild hankering, then you'll drop the current work. There are delirious moments when you're blessed with a profusion of ideas, and you'll want to ride on that momentum. It certainly beats staggering aimlessly in the desert during those recurring dry spells.

If you temporarily halt your current work and lurch into the next, be mindful. Your ideas are like snowballs: they usually accelerate in pace and graduate in complexity. If you stop in the middle of study #1 and move on to studies #2 and #3, you might never return to #1 because you've outgrown the concept. You've assimilated what you've learned from study #1 and moved beyond it. How wonderful! This is one of the reasons for working in a series.

But in addition to providing foundations of learning, your studies also become your own personal reference library. They reflect how and what you were thinking and what decisions were made in your designing process. They become illustrations of your conscious choices to date. They also display your natural (unconscious) design tendencies.

By keeping each study compositionally coherent and by working each study through to completion—regardless of how simple—you advance your skills in two areas: resolution and unity. Even if it's resolution of a very simple idea, by working through to the finish (all the way to the binding), you increase your ability to see and make decisions regarding your work as a unified whole. As your design decisions increase, your ability to make them improves. You make them with greater ease, with less emotional torment.

Suggestions for Getting Unstuck

So, you've done two studies and you're stuck. The ideas evaporated. Now what? If I suggest you have the freedom to do anything, the magnitude of this can leave you either hyperventilating or comatose. So, here are some practical suggestions for getting unstuck. (Also review "Observations on the Creative Process" on pages 34–48.)

- Increase the restrictions. Operating within tighter boundaries can force some astounding creativity. Sometimes the breadth and depth of imaginative ideas are directly proportional to the limitations. Remember those brilliant prison-camp shenanigans from the movie "The Great Escape"? Closer to home, Round Robins are marvelous examples of creativity overcoming rigid, imposed rules. Some sample restrictions:
  - Use only two contrasting colors.
  - Make it asymmetric.
  - Divide some of the templates in half, in quarters, in tenths.
  - Use only triangles, but many sizes.
  - Use cheater fabric in unexpected applications.
  - Use only the ugliest fabric in your collection.
  - Randomly open a quilt book and make the quilt on that page.

By the way, just because you start with an artificial rule doesn't mean you must stick with it. Once your creative juices start to flow and they move you away from the imposed rule, unload the silly thing. Remember, it's just a tool to jump-start your ideas, not a clause in your prenuptial agreement.

By its very nature, working in a series is itself a restrictive device. New variations are introduced to develop an idea or an association of ideas, but they all refer to the original one.

- Depart from normal. Whatever your natural inclination, deviate or do the opposite. If you always use blue, go with autumn hues. If you always use 90° angles, try spikes or slashes. If your quilts always look scrappy, limit yourself to three solids throughout. If you always use florals, try plaids. It's fair to assume you'll definitely learn something from these departures. You'll learn about the new fabric and its idiosyncrasies, and you'll learn about yourself in the adaptation.

- Start another series. Ideas attract ideas, so keep them coming. There's no law mandating you must work on one series or one quilt uninterrupted, from beginning to end, before approaching another.

  Personally, I find working simultaneously on a variety of quilts relaxing and appropriate to my style. When I'm stalled or trapped in some tedious marathon assembly, I leave it and go play with another quilt, then shuffle back and forth. Resumption of the quilt in suspense depends on my ability or willingness. There are times when mindless, marathon assemblies suit my temperament. Or the light bulb appears overhead, allowing my return to the problem quilt to tackle that original sticking place with bravado. The law of least resistance often is a favorable operative.

- Borrow from another quilt's success. Rather than copying piece by piece, make modifications by reversing the values or changing the sequence. By focusing on these derivations, you get to analyze someone else's design process and problem-solving techniques. Borrowing ideas, whether intentional or not, is rampant throughout every enterprise—commerce, sports, the arts, and especially advertising. Learning from the successes of others is part of the human legacy. During the early stages of their development, many masters—including Picasso, Balanchine, and Brahms—borrowed from their predecessors. In art, writing, and music classes today, assignments still include studying the masters through mimicry.

✔ Revive yourself through your idea book, file, pile, or junk drawer. I have all the above because I'm not very organized. However, I'm most proud of The List. Taped to my studio door is a list of quilt ideas I plan to make in my lifetime. The list gets longer, but it never fails to excite me toward at least one project I need to start right now. (I've disciplined myself to never, never look at this list late at night.)

Similarly, your series can be enhanced by adapting a long-standing idea. The time may be ripe for its incarnation in your current series or within several series. This happened with the Mandala Series. The mandala idea was superimposed over the block studies.

✔ Unless you're developing your series in secrecy, ask someone for suggestions. You might cherish their advice or hate it. If the advice is suspect, at least you know what you don't want to do. That's an increase in knowledge.

The advantage to this tactic doesn't necessarily rest with the actual advice offered. More often than not, others see things in your work that you don't and make passing comments about them. These casual perceptions are precious bits of information and are appreciably more valuable than the advice that follows.

Honest or even skewed opinions from another perspective are provocative learning. You're under no obligation to adhere to the advice if it's unsuitable. It's still your quilt, still your series. Whether you concur with the outsiders or not, whatever you hear will get you going, one way or another. Muses, those catalysts for action, often come oddly disguised.

✔ Listen to music that develops themes on a grand scale. Bach's *Brandenburg Concertos* or *Goldberg Variations* (actually anything and everything Bach) are great for probing idea development and construction. Or, try the Chopin groupings, such as his sonatas or nocturnes.

Even if your musicianship is nil (I fall into this category), and you've lost your music decoder ring, I'm convinced that music can be absorbed into the system like vitamins. Subliminally, it helps you sense how an idea develops and unfolds. If one teensy piece of fabric is equivalent to one musical note, then …

When making studies within a contemporary context, there's the opportunity to experiment with technique and material …

✓ Learn from the experts. Look at successful visual work: paintings, vases, temples, tapestries. Thousands of years' worth of valuable aesthetic clues abound in books and museums. Analyze what was done to achieve these successes. Visit these treasures and figure them out. Refining your visual acuity is always a worthy investment of your time. If for nothing else, the sheer pleasure of viewing will nourish your spirit.

✓ Clean your studio. I can't tell you how many quilt ideas have come to mind when I've done this. Some forgotten piece of fabric retriggers that once bright idea that prompted its purchase. It remains a good idea, so I start in. Sorting through retired projects makes me laugh and reminds me of where an idea turned sour. But now I have a clear answer for revision. Or maybe it's still hopeless, but laughing shakes things up and allows me to approach the world with a relaxed spirit. This friendly internal atmosphere is more conducive for nurturing ideas than wallowing in a desolate muddle. Of course, a clean studio is itself inspiration.

✓ According to the Book of Genesis, God's series of impressive creations started with a word. So, if it's good enough for God, it ought to be good enough for you. Go find some words, some phrases. Poets are wordsmiths, so starting in this domain makes sense. Dust off old books or discover new talent. Not all the great poets are dead. Many are alive and well and would welcome new fans.

The important books of wisdom—the Upanishads, the Bible, the Koran, the Tao Te Ching—should have at least one nugget of inspiration within their pages. But any word source will do. Sometimes you don't need to get past the titles. Search wherever it pleases you.

✓ Make a pilgrimage. Revisit your life. Here's a vast store of reference material that no one else can tap into. Since this is an expansive topic to explore, it may be easier to isolate selected short subjects, such as a family vacation, the second grade, your first heartbreak, a breakthrough experience of any kind. There's a quilt in there somewhere.

✓ Sit still, be quiet. This is a valuable tactic for almost anything in your life, not just quilt ideas.

Designing

Making studies is an independent endeavor: you're on your own, left to your own devices. You deliberately put yourself in a situation that summons your skills, your fantasies, and your creativity. This is your private mystery-quilt class, with the teacher and student being one and the same.

Making studies is exploratory and experimental. Anything you discover and do for the first time, without benefit of packaged patterns or specific guidance, is exploratory and experimental for you, regardless of what's transpired elsewhere in Quilt World.

When making studies within a contemporary context, there's the opportunity to experiment with technique and material, such as loose thread, plastic wrap, and staples, and to explore the boundaries of content, for example, the symbolic, surreal, or metaphysical aspects. Eventually, however, the working and doing, the experimenting and exploring must entertain the principles of visual design. Whether the approach is traditional, contemporary, or somewhere in between, making visual studies examines our personal understanding and assumptions about design.

In quiltmaking, to design is to organize material in ways that fulfill function and bring visual satisfaction. Transforming fabric into table runners, lap quilts, wall hangings, or other projects fulfills the functionary aspect. Form becomes function and the left brain cheers. And although visual satisfaction is totally subjective—and therefore nobody's business but the maker's—it's still possible to discuss design concepts without personal trespass.

When we design, we manipulate materials to express our ideas. Included in the concept of our ideas are their sources: the intellect and the subconscious.

When we design, we tap our subconscious, a potent potpourri of experiences, assimilated learnings, latent images, intuition, emotional impressions—all sorts of weird and wonderful stuff. The essence of how and what we perceive, gathered for the purpose of designing, is defined and structured by this concoction. Scholarship in fine or graphic arts may polish your skills and increase your intellectual pool, but these, too, are ingredients that blend into the mixture. When we design, we delve into ourselves for insight. We know we hit pay dirt when we're moved, when we react to what we're doing.

Very often, outside influences affect what we do, not because the input is better, more august, or more appropriate, but because of what is triggered within us. Our unconscious recognition and kinship of its resonance prompts us to act.

Design Concepts

The basic elements of quiltmaking design are form, color, and space. Because of the way quilts are constructed, these elements are inherent to the task of quiltmaking. No conscious effort is required, and no one forgets to include them. It's a done deal.

All successful design begins with the ability to see, to perceive. Perception not only ascertains what's there, but also divines what's implied. What we perceive in design are relationships, the relationships of form, color, and space, and the relationships of these elements with each other and the whole.

The theories of these relationships are the principles of design. Whether conscious or not, if particular effects are desired in a quilt, we always address these principles, usually considered to be unity, balance, emphasis, and rhythm. The personal interpretation of these principles lends animation, personality, and style to our quilts.

The Principles of Design: A General Consensus

The principles of design are so interrelated that isolating each for discussion is nearly impossible. They are addressed here in shorthand to prevent you from dozing off. This discussion provides a broad sense of how we deal with these principles. It's not a definitive account of the entire design process. As we know, the left brain has a terrible time explaining the operations of the right brain.

Also, be suspicious of this guy, General Consensus. He and a group of expert authorities once ridiculed Monet, Picasso, van Gogh, Matisse, Degas, and many others. Hence, I encourage individual assessments and challenges of all that follows.

Unity

THE CONCEPT: Design elements of form, color, and space are integrated and perceived as congruous, although each contributes something different to the whole. There is a common bond, element, or thread—whether implied or actual—that holds the composition together. Taken altogether, the piece makes visual sense. The variety and diversity of individual components, or the maelstrom of movement, are complementary. Aimlessness or chaos is averted. The composition presents itself as a whole. The residual image is comprehensive and coherent, and no part is passive within the quilt.

MANEUVERS: Integrate; let the quilt evolve. Use same, similar, or gradations of shapes and/or colors, and have them correspond to the whole. Elements are repeated, though not necessarily verbatim. See and develop your quilt as a composition, not a collection of parts that will need containment later. Assembling units into one large physical piece is not equivalent to a visual composition.

... mix has its limits, and we know the rodeo bandanna doesn't work with the silk crepe dress. When we switch shoes or earrings ... we are designing ourselves with unity in mind.

Perils: Too much unity makes the quilt static, overly tended. The development of a larger concept is truncated. Too little unity and haphazard jumbles predominate; ideas seem adrift. Disparate elements remain disparate. The disorganization doesn't satisfy a visual purpose.

Reality Check: When we dress ourselves for special occasions, we employ the principles of unity. Even if we don't use the same color and material from head to toe, we can still feel coordinated by a mix of elements. But the mix has its limits, and we know the rodeo bandanna doesn't work with the silk crepe dress. When we switch shoes or earrings and perhaps even run through a battery of other possibilities, we are designing ourselves with unity in mind. As we add, switch, and subtract, we check constantly in the mirror to see if the different parts contribute to the overall look we wish to attain.

Balance

The Concept: Balance is usually achieved through contrast of elements, their relational proportions, size, and placement. It confers stability, either suggested or actual. Tension is created and resolved, even if partially. What's available to the eye is generally characterized in terms of symmetry or asymmetry.

Maneuvers: Contrast, add, subtract, divide, multiply, eliminate, subdue, repeat, switch, increase, strengthen, exaggerate, weaken, substitute, relocate, replace. Just move something somewhere else, even out of the quilt.

Perils: Too much balance makes the quilt predictable. Too little creates unresolved tension. The quilt feels awkward, usually heavy, without breathing spaces.

Reality Check: When cooking, we try to achieve a balance in flavors. Just because we've used a cup of red wine in the stew doesn't mean we also use a cup of sage and a cup of thyme. We know through experience that balance doesn't necessarily mean equal measure.

Rhythm

The Concept: Rhythm is usually achieved through repetition and perceived movements or transitions of elements. Repetition may be dynamic or subtle, occur at regular or irregular intervals, and be of the same or different duration. Simultaneous, contrapuntal rhythms can produce stunning effects.

The ordering and manipulation of rhythm throughout a quilt is probably the most elaborate of all designing schemes. Frequently, I see it as trying to forge a melody line from a collection of assorted notes. The result can range from a sensitive, simple folk tune like "Shenandoah," sung by Harry Belafonte without accompaniment, to the rich complexities of Mozart's *The Magic Flute*. Both pieces are breathtaking. I've not come close to achieving the characteristics of either, but they do provide a world of immanent possibilities and compelling ideas to toy with.

MANEUVERS: Contrast, repeat, suspend, diverge, resume, converge, ripple, weave, reverse, strengthen, compress, weaken, substitute. Run them parallel, at counterpoint, or through another rhythm.

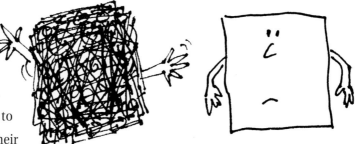

PERILS: Too much rhythm yields confusion; too little results in a lifeless quilt.

REALITY CHECK: When designing our gardens, we try to arrange the different plants to their best advantage and to integrate them so they enhance each other. We also look at location, which carries its own sense of space and interval. Whether we place only cosmos on the berm, randomly intersperse them with mignonette and bachelor's button, or plant only masses of hostas or ornamental grasses, we bring visual rhythm to the garden.

Emphasis

THE CONCEPT: Achieve emphasis by giving prominence to a particular element or area. This is usually done through contrast of color, value, size, texture, detailing, or placement.

MANEUVERS: Contrast, location, proportion, surprise.

PERILS: Too much emphasis dilutes impact; too little produces a vapid appearance.

REALITY CHECK: A solitary kite in the sky. Booming cannons in Tchaikovsky's "1812 Overture." A dash of hot sauce on scrambled eggs.

When we create something born of our own spirit, it's magic.

Understanding and analyzing these design principles assumes importance when we're stuck. When I'm stuck, I want to know how I got there and the options for getting out. I don't want only one option. Just as a greater understanding of fabric and color broadens and strengthens our skills in using them, so it is with design principles. The greater our knowledge, the greater our flexibility and fluency in managing materials and producing desired effects in our quilts. The principles of design are not goals. They are intimate allies, and in befriending them, our chances improve for making the kinds of quilts we alone see in our imagination.

Describe your quilts using adjectives or descriptive phrases. Do your quilts say something about themselves, or do they just sit there? For your future quilts, what would you like them to say? If you can answer this question, then your task is to determine how to express it. When we create something born of our own spirit, it's magic.

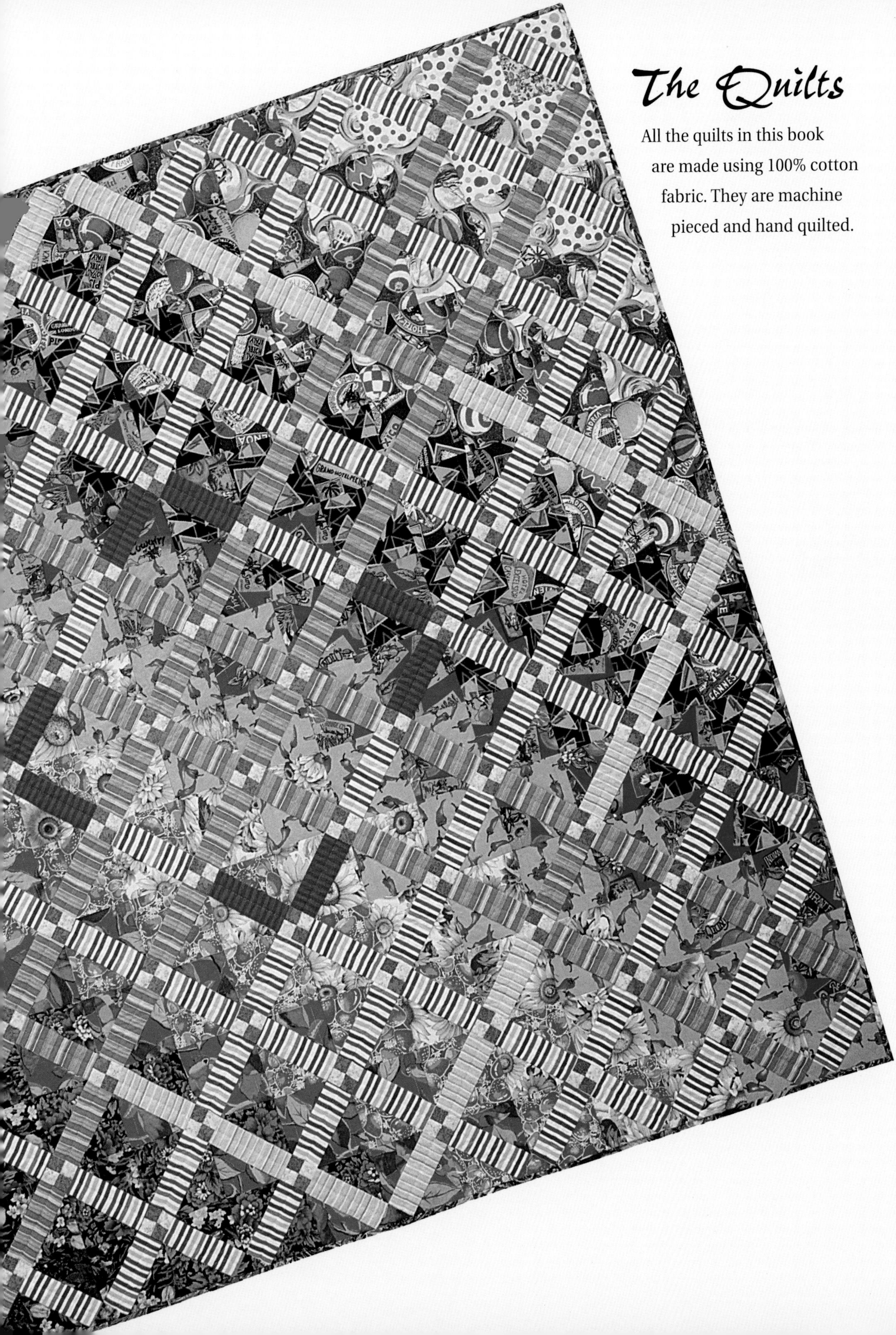

The Quilts

All the quilts in this book
are made using 100% cotton
fabric. They are machine
pieced and hand quilted.

The venerable Nine Patch block is my candidate for the most widely used and identifiable unit in Quilt World. In all probability, it's the first block attempted by most beginning quilters. The simple checkerboard arrangement of equal, alternating patches immediately establishes patterns of pure form and pure rhythm.

More than the circle, square, triangle, swirl, and cruciform (all of which carry symbolic, archetypal weight), the checkerboard may be seen as one of the first patterns of nonrepresentational elements. The checkerboard is a rare occurrence in nature, yet this design scheme is universal. Perhaps it developed as a result of simple plaiting. Remember the place mats woven from colored strips of construction paper that we made in kindergarten? Voilà, the basic checkerboard! See page 93 for block assembly illustration.

The Broken Dish block is another basic division of the square. The square is divided twice diagonally from corner to corner, forming four symmetric triangles. See page 93 for block assembly illustration.

Connecticut Variation is a vintage block pattern, again of simple components: Four Patch, Broken Dish, and Square within a Square. Just as literature attributes its wealth to a handful of simple story lines, the yield of quilt variations is broader with very basic blocks. See page 93 for block assembly illustration.

The Shoo Fly block is a variation on the basic Nine Patch. The corner squares are cut in half diagonally, introducing not only triangle shapes, but another visual direction as well. Churn Dash is a variation of Shoo Fly, where the remaining outside squares are cut in half, creating rectangles with their long edges parallel to the block's outer edges. See page 93 for block assembly illustration.

I'd be floored if this block name, "Odd Couple," is discovered in any hallowed quilt canon. I made it up. Perhaps the block itself has a previously assigned name, but I've yet to discover it. Perhaps it's too simple a composition. (It's basically a one patch, sashed on two sides and with one cornerstone.) See page 93 for block assembly illustration.

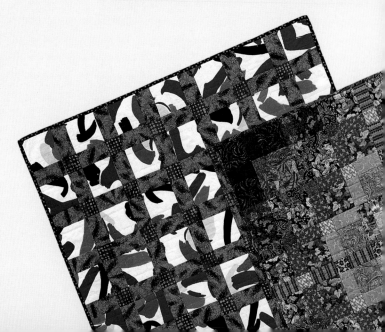

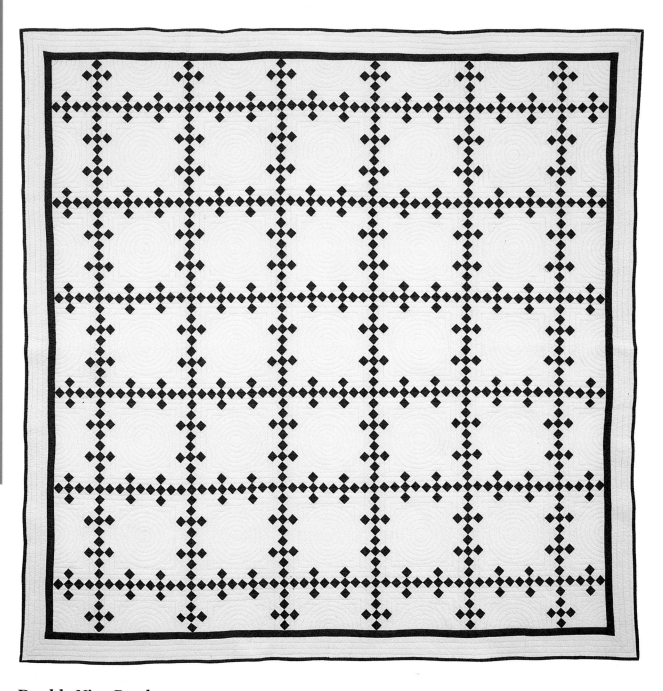

Double Nine Patch *by Tonye Phillips, 1995, Camp Sherman, Oregon, 84" x 84" (Collection of the artist).*
Construction: *Double Nine Patch blocks, alternating plain blocks; set on point, with triple, mitered border.*

This beautiful quilt, created by my friend, quilting confidante, and neighbor, Tonye Phillips, is an exquisite example of the Double Nine Patch in a traditional setting. The blue print reads as a solid, providing crisp delineations of a blue network intersecting over a field of white. The quilting pattern of concentric circles provides counterpoint to the linear grid work.

In my collection of quilt pictures torn from assorted magazines, vintage versions of this Double Nine Patch reappear time and again. Rendered in every color—olive, red, orange, yellow, powder blue—I adore them all. Their quiet, simple orderliness gets to me, plain and simple.

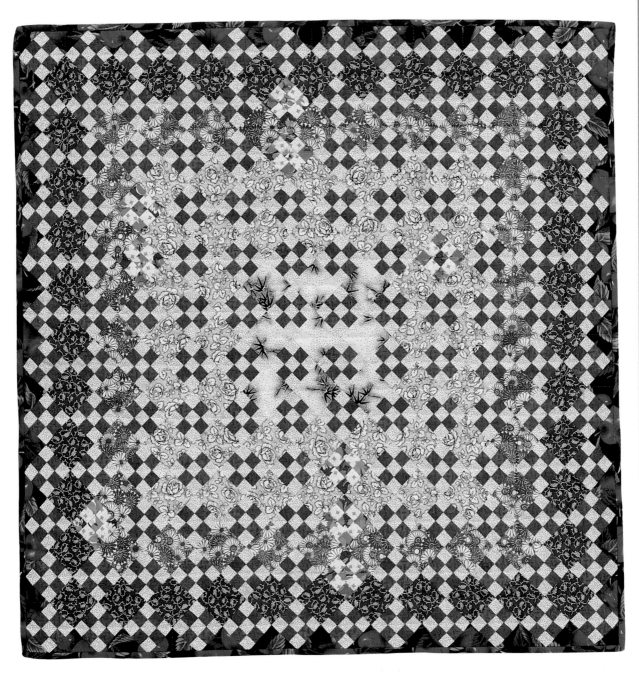

Nine Patch Study #3 *by Andrea Balosky, 1993, Camp Sherman, Oregon, 31" x 31" (Collection of Cathi Howell).*

Construction: Single Nine Patch blocks with alternating plain blocks; set on point.

This quilt is a study of gradating light to dark values, moving from the center outward. The value changes occur across the alternating blocks, while the color scheme of most of the Nine Patch blocks remains constant.

To keep the units somewhat fluid, the dominant colors in the Nine Patch blocks blend from claret to bruise blue. The very dark print at the quilt edges halts the gradation without imprisoning it. The deep, brooding greens and reds of the print read as dark, but provide a respite of color. I interspersed occasional Nine Patch blocks in a tropical print to relieve the structural repetition, reversing the values.

Zona Rosa *by Andrea Balosky, 1994, Camp Sherman, Oregon, 51" x 51".*

Construction: *Single Nine Patch blocks with alternating plain blocks; set on point.*

In the late sixties, I studied in Mexico City. While searching for more suitable accommodations, I lived briefly in a small hotel called the Hotel Londres. The less expensive rooms were at the back, and to get there, I had to cross the hotel's large central, enclosed courtyard. I recall neither the color scheme nor the pattern of the tile work in the courtyard, but this quilt is reminiscent of what I vaguely remember. The hotel is located in a district known as Zona Rosa.

I designed "Zona Rosa" from the center outward. I preselected the central stained glass and coral/rose fabrics from my inventory. I added all the other fabrics after the initial layout to complement and shape the courtyard. I substituted colors and prints as I ran out of original fabrics. I like the way the Nine Patch blocks float against the light alternating blocks, then become absorbed at the edges by the dark alternating blocks.

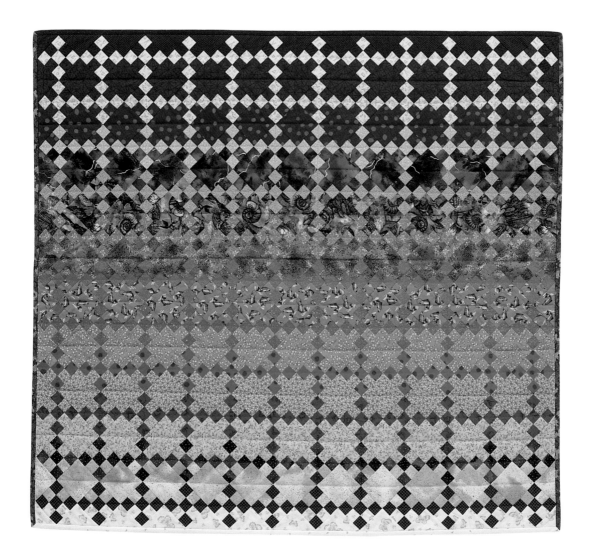

Sundown *by Andrea Balosky, 1995, Camp Sherman, Oregon, 51" x 47".*

Construction: *Single Nine Patch blocks with alternating plain blocks; set on point.*

Some of the tenderest memories of my childhood in Hawaii involve the large, wide front porch of my grandparents' home on Panui Lane. In the early evenings after work (called "pau hana time"), family and neighbors would gather on the steps and porch to relax, easing into the remainder of the day.

Our neighbor across the lane would saunter over to the house, greeting everyone with kisses, a broad smile, and a few words. He'd settle into his favorite spot against one of the pillars, take a sip of beer, strum a few practice chords on his old guitar, then tune the strings. He'd smile again—an all-encompassing, toothless smile—then start to play a particular style of Hawaiian music called "slack key."

Although it can be perky and upbeat, slack key is usually played slow. The strings are individually plucked and hammered, producing an overall sound that is soothing and hypnotic. Sometimes we porch people would sing and play along, harmonizing and making music as best we could.

He was a gifted musician, a very gentle, modest man, who was loved by everyone in the neighborhood. This quilt is made in memory of a sweet time in my life, the sweet time of day, Panui Lane, my family, and the man known to everyone as "Sundown."

This simple study involves the gradations of two color families: red and blue. The blue squares gradate from light at the bottom to dark at the top; the reds gradate from light at the top to dark at the bottom. Somewhere in the middle, the gradations interlock. The value distinctions are lost, resulting in a blurred, hazy effect, which is further accentuated by the high-contrast punch at the top and bottom.

Abstractly, the lightest gradation of red (here white-pink) appears like stars against a midnight sky. The medium reds and blues allude to horizon and sunset. All fabrics were recruited from my inventory, hence the gradations aren't perfect, but these fabrics lend a quality to the quilt that I welcome more than flawless matching.

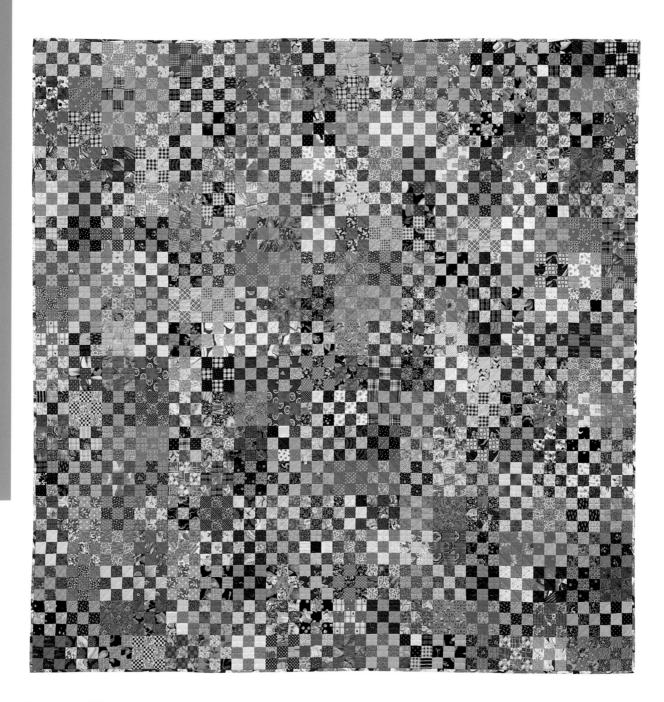

Two the Nines *by Andrea Balosky, 1994, Camp Sherman, Oregon, 78½" x 78½".*

Construction: *Single Nine Patch blocks.*

I love scrap quilts. I love making them, and I love looking at them. Because of the random selection and placement of bits of fabric, the eye roams across the quilt landscape in an attempt to make some sense of the arrangement. This visual wandering is curiously contemplative, despite the fact that scrap quilts have a busy visual connotation.

I learn a lot about color and print combinations from viewing scrap quilts. The arbitrary arrangement creates a framework for discovering color alliances that are surprising and also peculiar.

Intrinsic to scrap quilts is a lurking sense that all is not quite right, that absolute visual resolution is lacking. To some degree, the effect of some scrap quilts is slightly screwball, hovering on the brink of zaniness. This quirk factor significantly contributes to making scrap quilts permanent fixtures in my quilting life.

Indian Summer *by Andrea Balosky, 1995, Camp Sherman, Oregon, 31" x 32".*

Construction: *Nine Patch variation blocks with sashing and mini-border.*

"Indian Summer" shows a more relaxed approach to quiltmaking, reminiscent of the grassroots quilts of yesteryear. I cut the pieces freehand, without templates, and made no attempt to match most intersections.

Grassroots quilts endlessly fascinate me. Most of them are scrappy, and I normally refer to them in this category. Beyond the high energy of color, what's also attractive is the presence of the human hand. It's that special quality that differentiates the handmade from the mass-produced. Quiltmaking is an excellent example of this differentiation. So are handmade candles, hand-written letters, pen and ink sketches, hand-dipped chocolates, and homemade cookies. The arresting beauty of gentle un-

evenness resonates with a particular kind of energy that is both controlled and accommodated at precisely the same moment. There is enough controlled energy to repeat the required forms, yet this same energy is also relaxed enough to register the personal disposition of the maker at the moment of its making. Most anything handmade endures because of this endowment. It reveals the presence of the heart and hand.

In this quilt, there are nine blocks of the same Nine Patch variation. In each block, the center square is one piece. The corner squares are four-patch units, and the remaining squares are divided into two rectangles, with the long sides parallel to the edges of the block.

71

Fiesta Ware with Three Pinwheels *by Andrea Balosky, 1995, Camp Sherman, Oregon, 43½" x 43½".*

Construction: *Single Broken Dish blocks in quarter-turn rotations.*

Because of the block name, I wanted the traditional example for this series to suggest the idea of dishes. The burnished, vivid colors of Fiesta dishes provided inspiration for the hues I selected. The dinner-plate size block is also relevant to the idea. The pinwheels offer a visual shift, a departure from the expected.

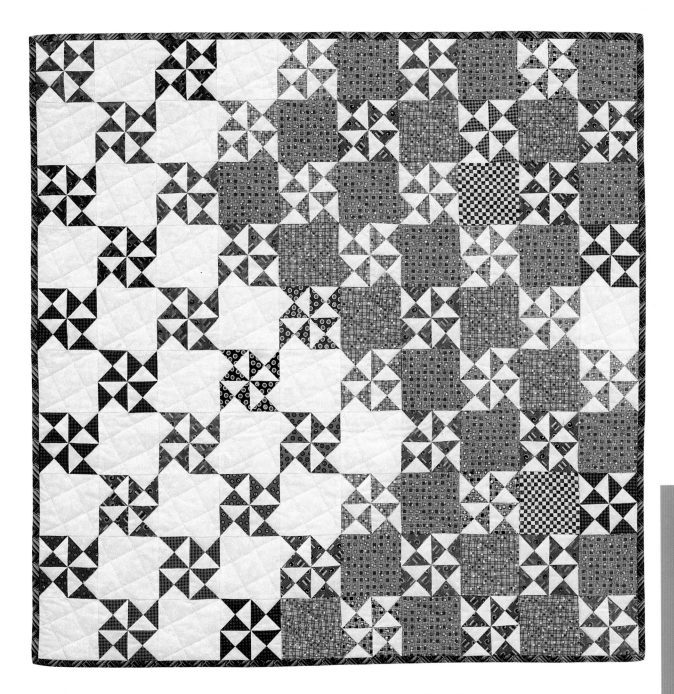

Anvil Chorus *by Andrea Balosky, 1995, Camp Sherman, Oregon, 40" x 40".*

Construction: *Four Broken Dish blocks combined to make each block, set with alternating plain blocks.*

Taken singly in alternating, high-contrast fabrics, the Broken Dish shapes look like little anvils.

"Anvil Chorus" is another exercise in having the basic block develop into something different from what is strictly rendered by its parts. When the Broken Dish blocks surround the plain block, the related fabrics blend, resulting in a new shape. Transformed, the new shape appears splayed and slightly skewed. The pinwheel shapes appear reversed on one side of the quilt from those on the other side. This combination of elements automatically imparts direction and movement.

Knowing that the new yellow shape moved in one direction and the new printed shape moved in another, I reckoned that, when side by side, they would appear to collide. I produced this study to see what that collision would look like.

Take Four *by Andrea Balosky, 1995, Camp Sherman, Oregon, 38" x 38".*

Construction: *Single Broken Dish blocks.*

I've always wanted to experiment with reassembling striped triangles into new squares. As with some studies, I am likely to explore further considerations of this concept before creating a fully expanded, comprehensive piece. One of the benefits of making this quilt was the joy of watching the development of the variations. It's the same simple pleasure as looking through a kaleidoscope. All the pieces fall into place without much effort, yielding wonderful surprises.

Cross-Currents Study #2 *by Andrea Balosky, 1994, Camp Sherman, Oregon, 74" x 74" (Collection of Debbie Myers).*

Construction: Single Broken Dish blocks on point, with sashing and nine-patch cornerstones. Each of the four central blocks is the Snail's Trail pattern.

I made the Snail's Trail blocks initially as extraneous studies, testing the visual possibilities of the trails in value gradations. I made them with no end product in mind. At the same time, I was interested in working with stripes, a generally underutilized fabric. I embarked on the Cross-Currents series to explore the integration of these two visual ideas.

Combined, the four Snail's Trail blocks give the feeling of spinning outward. Keeping the field hue

somewhat neutral, the colors gain significance at the corners. Combined with the spinning center, the quilt seems to be at the mercy of centrifugal forces, pushing the colors outward off the edge of the quilt. There's a tendency to want to rearrange the colors, to pull them center stage, where they "ought" to be.

Some of the nine-patch cornerstones are leftovers from "Nine Patch Study #3" on page 67.

Cross-Currents Study #3 *by Andrea Balosky, 1995, Camp Sherman, Oregon, 74" x 74".*

Construction: *Single Broken Dish blocks on point, with sashing and nine-patch cornerstones.*

If "Cross-Currents Study #2" (page75) is nearly void of color, then "Cross-Currents Study #3" is an overdose. A progressive advance of vivid colors runs diagonally across the quilt. Streaming through these color changes, the four-patch cornerstones, normally stalwart and virtuous, lose their stability and shimmer on the surface.

As in "Cross-Currents Study #2," the striped sashing doesn't operate as an adhesive to link blocks together. Rather, it performs as an equal, visual partner to the blocks and provides a vehicle for color and pattern interactions.

Broken Dish Series

The Promise of Seeds *(Gaia Mandala, Mandala Series) by Andrea Balosky, 1995, Camp Sherman, Oregon, 43" x 43".*

Construction: Single Broken Dish blocks with alternating plain blocks.

The fabric prints contour the overall quilt design. I did not selectively cut each fabric piece, but cut the fabric according to the size needed and used them "as is." Obviously, they were selectively placed.

In early spring, when making this quilt, I listened to my intrepid-gardener husband rattle his treasured seed packets in preparation for the growing season.

There is great anticipation, hope, and dream fulfillment in the rituals of the first planting.

In addition, this quilt pays homage to the preciousness of biodiversity and to those highly committed people involved in ad hoc seed exchange and seed-preservation programs.

Egg Hunt *by Andrea Balosky, 1994, Camp Sherman, Oregon, 40½" x 40½".*

Construction: *Single Connecticut Variation blocks; assembled by units into horizontal rows, then sewn together.*

Within this quilt is a charming fabric of painted Easter eggs. I chose it first and selected the other fabrics as companions. Once assembled, however, the Easter eggs lost their identity and impact; hence, the name.

And yes, there is a mistake in this quilt. It would be wonderful to say the mistake was intentional, that I was maintaining the tradition of incorporating a small error in the quilt's creation. But no, I didn't notice the mistake until halfway through the hand-quilting stage.

Fragments *by Andrea Balosky, 1994, Camp Sherman, Oregon, 40½" x 40½".*

Construction: *Single Connecticut Variation blocks. Constructed in the same manner as "Egg Hunt" on page 78.*

While making "Egg Hunt," I noticed that I liked the visual aspect of the partially assembled squares awaiting completion. "Fragments" is a study of pastiche squares amidst and emerging from the rubble. The close color values accentuate the fragmentation.

Campostelle *by Andrea Balosky, 1995, Camp Sherman, Oregon, 49" x 49".*

Composition: *Single Connecticut Variation blocks. Constructed in the same manner as "Egg Hunt" on page 78.*

I designed "Campostelle" ("Field of Stars") for those quiltmakers whose fabric stash bears a conservative stamp. (Perhaps the intent is to add more exotic and provocative prints to the collection, but at the moment, it still looks unadventuresome.)

Without aborting one's collection, it's possible to manipulate existing sober prints into a dashing configuration. The success of this quilt lies with the manipulation of value, regardless of the color.

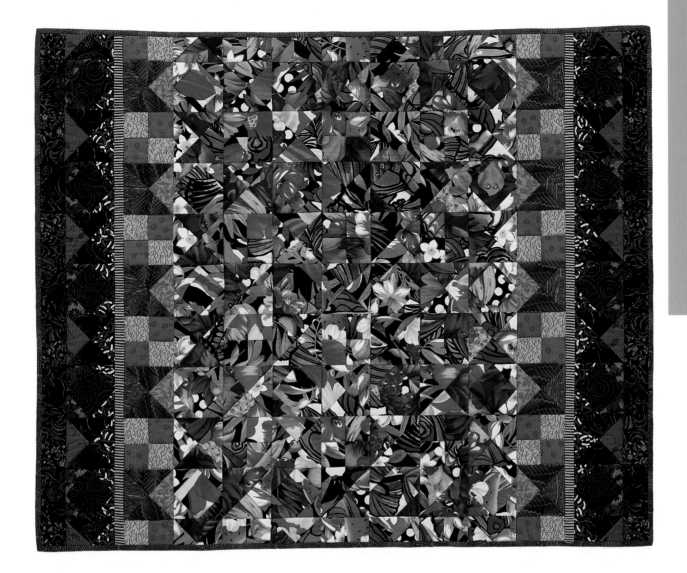

Lucia di Luau *by Andrea Balosky, 1995, Camp Sherman, Oregon, 50" x 40".*

Construction: *Single Connecticut Variation blocks. Constructed in the same manner as "Egg Hunt" on page 78, with added vertical strips.*

"Lucia" started at the edges, not knowing it would end up there. What I originally produced appeared so forbiddingly formal (and so operatic!) that I decided to give it a complete turnaround. I recruited as many tropicals as seemed appropriate and applied massive infusions of tropical punch. The quilt then transformed into "Lucia di Luau."

Apostrophe Blue *by Andrea Balosky, 1995, Camp Sherman, Oregon, 49" x 49".*

Construction: *Single Connecticut Variation blocks. Constructed in the same manner as "Egg Hunt" on page 78, without the edge rows, but with added borders.*

"Apostrophe Blue" is an exercise in adapting the angular qualities of the Connecticut Variation block to a configuration that is perceived as more curved and sweeping. It's also an attempt to make a quilt that is somewhat bluish. (Blue is the color I use least.)

Casa di Riposo *by Andrea Balosky, 1995, Camp Sherman, Oregon, 46" x 46" (Private collection).*

Construction: *Single Shoo Fly blocks on point, with alternating plain blocks; single border with cornerstones.*

This quilt evokes an old-world charm in both coloration and layout. The quilt name is associated with the opera composer Giuseppe Verdi. He died in 1901, leaving almost his entire estate to the establishment and maintenance of Casa di Riposo, a retirement home in Milan for musicians and singers.

I've not visited there, but in my fantasy, I imagine Casa di Riposo as a place of repose, of dignified grace, filled with old roses and grape arbors, and detailed with wrought-iron ornamentation. I read later that some of these elements are indeed present.

Gatekeepers *(Dorje Mandala, Mandala Series) by Andrea Balosky, 1995, Camp Sherman, Oregon, 44½" x 44½" (Private collection).*

Construction: *Combinations of Shoo Fly, Churn Dash, and variations.*

"Gatekeepers" is part of the Mandala Series. The red gates represent a threshold, a place of symbolic readiness where one's spiritual path embraces alternate perceptions of reality. Since the journey inward is clearly unknown, one consciously accepts the probability of encountering strange beasts and other wonders along the way and welcomes the transformation resulting from the experience.

Five chartreuse center squares represent a cross-sectional view of the dorje, a ritual instrument used principally by Tibetan Buddhists. It represents the thunderbolt of enlightenment and wisdom.

The Blue Quilt *by Andrea Balosky, 1995, Camp Sherman, Oregon, 44" x 44" (Private collection).*

Construction: *Single Churn Dash blocks.*

Of all the colors, I use blue the least, leaning toward the warmer side of the spectrum. While preparing for this book, I reminded myself to include blue in the quilt studies, to sustain a full color range. "The Blue Quilt" fully intended to live up to its name, but this is the result.

When four Churn Dash blocks are placed next to each other, the half-square triangle units create a Broken Dish square on point. "The Blue Quilt" emphasizes this secondary pattern.

Ring of Fire (P & B Mandala, Mandala Series) by Andrea Balosky, 1995, Camp Sherman, Oregon, 40½" x 40½" (P & B Textiles, Inc., Corporate Collection).

Construction: Shoo Fly blocks. All the fabrics in "Ring of Fire" were provided by P & B Textiles.

"Ring of Fire" is part of the Mandala Series. It pays homage to Siva, a principal god in Hinduism. Siva is most frequently portrayed performing the universal dance of life, caught in a moment of one-footed balance, drum in one hand and skull in the other, surrounded by a ring of flames. The dancing Siva is fraught with symbolic imagery, of which there are myriad interpretations. They're all appropriate, the interpretation being exactly suited to the inquiry or inquirer.

Jerry's Garden *(Gaia Mandala II, Mandala Series) by Andrea Balosky, 1995, Camp Sherman, Oregon, 40½" x 40½".*

Construction: *Shoo Fly and Churn Dash blocks.*

"Jerry's Garden" is part of the Mandala Series. Each year, my husband Jerry pours his heart and soul into his garden. Our vegetable garden hosts many flowers as treats for the eye.

Summer always seems to be late in coming here in the foothills of the Oregon Cascades. At the peak of the summer (according to the calendar), our spring flowers are at full strength. The blooms and warm colors of real summer are still just glimmers of hope, because frost comes early too.

The dark greens in this quilt allude to the beauty of our surrounding ponderosa pines. Unfortunately, these tall trees provide more shade than is desirable for gardening.

R. D. *by Andrea Balosky, 1995, Camp Sherman, Oregon, 40½" x 40½".*

Construction: *Single Odd Couple blocks.*

"R. D." is a simple, unmanipulated repeat of the Odd Couple block. Obviously, when set side by side, the open-endedness of the Odd Couple disappears and becomes the veritable one patch, with conventional sashing and cornerstones. The featured fabric of the one patch saves the repeated format from tedium, with its large, multicolored brushstrokes, spontaneous and gestural.

Vespers *(Vespers Mandala, Mandala Series) by Andrea Balosky, 1995, Camp Sherman, Oregon, 40" x 40".*

Construction: *Single Odd Couple blocks.*

As with all the other studies in the Mandala Series, "Vespers" was not assembled in units. I selected and placed single pieces, working from the center and extending outward.

Within Christianity, Vespers is a prescribed time of evening prayer, also known as Evensong. The words themselves dictate the character of this study, hushed and subdued. Of course, the cruciform is central to the study, both symbolically and literally.

Dome Epais le Jasmin *by Andrea Balosky, 1995, Camp Sherman, Oregon, 41" x 32".*

Construction: *Single Odd Couple blocks with random rotations.*

While working on this piece, a CD of opera extracts was playing. I was drawn to the selection "Dome Epais le Jasmin" from *Lakme*. It's a gorgeous duet in which Lakme and her servant go to bathe in a beautiful secluded area. The music describes the setting as a river with a thick canopy of jasmine and roses. Although I hadn't intended to create a graphic representation of this place, the music affected my work. I suspect this study is also influenced by the proliferation of Impressionistic quilts currently in vogue. Just goes to prove I'm not immune to visual cross-infections.

Flying Down to Rio *by Andrea Balosky, 1995, Camp Sherman, Oregon, 44" x 44".*

Construction: *Single Odd Couple blocks in quarter-turn rotations. I added an extra row of pieced large squares and rectangles to surround the quilt.*

At first glance, "Flying Down to Rio" doesn't appear to fit this series. It looks different because all the original templates are subdivided. The large square is divided into one large unit and four smaller ones. The small square is divided into one large unit and two smaller ones. The rectangle is divided into two large and two small rectangles. All the subdivisions are "off square."

This study is my personal homage to Fred Astaire and Ginger Rogers. They first appeared together as a dance pair in the film, *Flying Down to Rio*, which ignited their own series of movies. Fred and Ginger made a total of ten films of incomparable dancing.

Diversity *by Andrea Balosky, 1995, Camp Sherman, Oregon, 54½" x 54½".*

Construction: *I assembled the tiny pieces comprising the large squares as units, but did not string-piece them. There is no reason other than I thought it would be more interesting. For those who need to know, there are sixty-four pieces in each unit. I compressed the widths of the rectangles and small squares for visual balance.*

I particularly enjoy scrap quilts made up of tiny pieces. The sheer number of conflicting prints and values seems to approach critical mass. This visual quality is intoxicating, aesthetic considerations aside.

"Diversity" is my testimonial to the strength and power of diversity—biological, social, and cultural. Nature's elegant balance and all that thrives within it deserves our respect.

Block Assembly

See the Nine Patch Series quilts on pages 66–71.

Nine Patch

See the Broken Dish Series quilts on pages 72–77.

Broken Dish

See the Shoo Fly/Churn Dash Series quilts on pages 83–87.

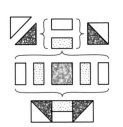

Shoo Fly

Churn Dash

See the Connecticut Variation Series quilts on pages 78–82. I constructed the Connecticut Variation quilts by units and rows, instead of blocks. Then I joined the rows to make the quilts.

Connecticut Variation

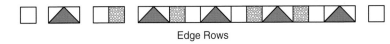

Edge Rows

Odd Rows

Even Rows

See the Odd Couple Series quilts on pages 88–92.

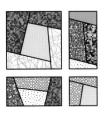

Odd Couple

Variation for "Flying Down to Rio" on page 91.

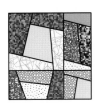

Bibliography

Arieti, Silvano. *Creativity: the Magic Synthesis.* New York: Basic Books, 1976.

Dewey, John. *Art as Experience.* New York: Putnam, 1934.

Campbell, Joseph. *The Power of the Myth.* New York: Doubleday, 1988.

———. *An Open Life.* New York: Harper & Row, 1990.

Capra, Fritjof. *The Tao of Physics.* New York: Bantam, 1977.

Fritz, Robert. *The Path of Least Resistance.* New York: Fawcett Columbine, 1984.

Edwards, Betty. *Drawing on the Right Side of the Brain.* Los Angeles: Tarcher, 1979.

———. *Drawing on the Artist Within.* New York: Simon & Schuster, 1986.

Ferguson, Marilyn. *The Aquarian Conspiracy.* Los Angeles: Tarcher, 1980.

Goldberg, Natalie. *Wild Mind: Living the Writer's Life.* New York: Bantam, 1990.

Goleman, Daniel, Paul Kaufman, and Michael Ray. *The Creative Spirit.* New York: Dutton, 1992.

John-Roger and Peter McWilliams. *Do It!* Los Angeles: Prelude, 1991.

Koberg, Don and Jim Bagnall. *The Universal Traveler.* Los Altos: William Kaufman, 1972.

Malcolm, Janet. "Profile: Forty-one False Starts," *The New Yorker,* July 11, 1994, 50–68.

Parnes, Sidney J. *The Magic of Your Mind.* Buffalo, N. Y.: Creative Education Foundation, 1981.

Ristad, Eloise. *A Soprano on Her Head.* Moab, Utah: Real People Press, 1982.

Rodman, Seldon. *Conversations with Artists.* New York: Capricorn, 1961.

Thompson, Charles "Chic." *What a Great Idea!* New York: Harper Collins, 1992.

Sargent, Walter. *The Enjoyment and Use of Color.* New York: Dover, 1964.

Stravinsky, Igor. *Poetics of Music.* Boston: Harvard University Press, 1942.

Von Oech, Roger. *A Whack on the Side of the Head.* New York: Warner, 1983.

———. *A Kick in the Seat of the Pants.* New York: Harper, 1986.

Music List

I listen to music while I work. I listen to everything. Despite all the pleasure that variety brings, invariably the music I turn to is opera. There's only one reason for preferring opera over the rest: its irrepressible beauty. I've seen opera referred to as "the most sublime music in the world of sublime music." Of course, I concur.

The following is a selected list of opera excerpts. They have one thing in common. In my listening history, at some moment, each piece signaled a new and expanded appreciation of what I understood as Opera. For this reason, I have a special fondness for them. This isn't my desert-island collection, although many are still favorites and could fall into this category.

"Chi mi frena" from *Lucia di Lammermoor* by Gaetano Donizetti

"Bella figlia dell'amore" from *Rigoletto* by Giuseppe Verdi

"Mon coeur s'ouvre à ta voix" from *Samson and Delilah* by Camille Saint-Saëns

"Va, pensiero" from *Nabucco* by Giuseppe Verdi

"Timor di me?' from *Il Travatore* by Giuseppe Verdi

"Soave sia il vento" from *Cosi Fan Tutti* by Wolfgang Amadeus Mozart

"Casta Diva" from *Norma* by Vincenzo Bellini

"Dove sono i bei momenti" from *Le Nozze di Figaro* by Wolfgang Amadeus Mozart

"Serbami ognor si fido" from *Semiramide* by Gioacchino Antonio Rossini

"Ah! Non credea mirarti" from *La Sonnambula* by Vincenzo Bellini

"Al dolce guidami castel natio" from *Anna Bolena* by Gaetano Donizetti

"Depuis le jour" from *Louise* by Gustave Charpentier

"Un ritratto? … Sventurato il cor che fida" from *La Straniera* by Vincenzo Bellini

"Oh! Rimembranza! … Oh non tremare … Oh di qual sei tu vittima" from *Norma* by Vincenzo Bellini

"Finale I" from *Fidelio* by Ludwig van Beethoven

Meet the Author

Through the best of good fortunes, Andrea Leong Balosky was born and raised in Hawaii. She is a self-taught quiltmaker and has been quilting off and on since 1964—mostly off. Since 1992, she has been self-apprenticing and is progressing somewhat. Being stranded in the woods, she ponders many things, including the paradoxes of the creative life. Her quilts have appeared in Quilt National '83, Houston's Labor of Love '92, the Sisters' Annual Outdoor Quilt Show, and *Quiltmaker* magazine. She is a happy member of East of the Cascades Quilters.

Andrea lives in Camp Sherman, Oregon, with her husband, Jerry, who builds birdhouses. They live amidst the ponderosa pine and many, many birdhouses. She listens to opera incessantly. They have two canaries, a pair of lovebirds, six chickens, one cat, a huge pond, and they time-share a Welsh terrier named Upton. Their current project is building a greenhouse from discarded windows.

Photo by Susan Dimitman

Publications and Products

Many titles are available at your local quilt shop.
For more information, write for a free color catalog
to That Patchwork Place, Inc., PO Box 118, Bothell,
WA 98041-0118 USA.

☎ U.S. and Canada, call **1-800-426-3126** for the
name and location of the quilt shop nearest you.
Int'l: 1-206-483-3313 **Fax:** 1-206-486-7596
E-mail: info@patchwork.com
Web: www.patchwork.com   12.96